BERKSHIRE OUTDOORS

Wildflowers

Wildflowers

OF THE
BERKSHIRE & TACONIC HILLS

BY JOSEPH G. STRAUCH, JR.
Photographs by the Author

Foreword by Steven Foster

BERKSHIRE HOUSE PUBLISHERS
Stockbridge, Massachusetts

The cover and text of this book was designed and composed by Jane McWhorter. Typefaces are Palatino and Helvetica. Cover photograph of *Hepatica acutifolia* (sharp-leaved hepatica) by Joseph G. Strauch, Jr. Map on p. XXIII by Ron Toelke Associates.

Editor: Sarah Novak.

Library of Congress Cataloging-in-Publication Data
Strauch, Joseph G.
Wildflowers of the Berkshire & Taconic Hills / by Joseph G. Strauch, Jr. ; photographs by the author.
p.   cm. — (Berkshire outdoors)
Includes bibliographical references (p.   ) and index.
ISBN 0-936399-66-X
Wild flowers—Massachusetts—Berkshire Hills—Identification. 2.
Wild flowers—Northeastern States—Identification. I. Title. II. Title: Wildflowers of the Berkshire and Taconic Hills. III. Series.
QK166.S75   1995
582.13′09744′1—dc20   94-41517
                                                        CIP

ISBN: 0-936399-66-X

Berkshire House Publishers
Box 297
Stockbridge, Massachusetts 01262

Manufactured in Singapore

First printing May 1995
10 9 8 7 6 5 4 3 2 1

To my wife,
whose support and encouragement
made this book possible.

CONTENTS

Color plates (species by color and plate number)
follow page 66

FOREWORD

To know a wildflower is to know yourself and your relationship to nature. There was a time when botany was a standard part of the secondary school curriculum. Now a class in botany, or plant sciences, as it has evolved in this era of molecular biology, is rare indeed. Rarer still is the individual who can name all of the plants that grow in his or her backyard. It is an irony in these days of environmental consciousness that we all too often appreciate wildflowers as little more than a blur of color fleeting by the car window. Stop the car. Take a moment for yourself. Observe. Enjoy the color, the beauty, the fragrance. Take a deep breath. Relax.

Twenty-one years ago, my career as a plantsman began in one moment at age seventeen when I stopped to look at and appreciate a wildflower.

"Stinking Benjamin. That's what my grandfather calls it," said my high school friend Colleen as we stopped to admire the nodding maroon blooms of a trillium (*Trillium erectum*).

"Smell it."

"I see how it got its name," I said.

"He says that they used to use the root as an aid in childbirth," she remembered. "Birthwort, they called it then."

My interest was further tweaked. I had been bitten by a bug. "I want to learn the names and uses of all the plants," I blurted.

Of course, I had no idea then, in the summer between my junior and senior years of high school in

Cumberland, Maine, that that statement would lead to a lifelong pursuit, to say nothing of a career. After all, the principal of my high school had a Ph.D. in botany, but there he was, a school administrator, far from the aquatic plants of his education.

Learning names and uses of plants is indeed a lifelong pursuit, one that can lead to any part of the world, back into history, or forward into the future.

Consider diversity. Compared with fewer than 3,000 species of birds, there are an estimated 250,000 to 800,000 species of flowering plants, half as yet unknown to science. At least 80,000 plant species have been used medicinally, at least as folk medicine. A chemist from a drug company recently noted that if a million medicinal chemists spent a million years synthesizing new compounds, they couldn't match the chemical diversity offered by Mother Nature in flowering plants. Humans rely on plants for food, clothing, shelter, medicine, fragrance, and even the oxygen we need to sustain life.

But if you stop for a moment to observe, study, or simply enjoy the beauty of a wildflower, you will soon discover that the more you learn about plants, the more you find there is to know. The excitement of seeing a plant for the first time — one that you have heard of, or one that is entirely new to you — is always fresh. Once you are bitten by this bug there is no turning back. The symptoms? Simply endless enjoyment, endless yearning to know more. If Roger Tory Peterson's first field guide had been on wildflowers rather than birds, we might see far more ads in nature magazines for hand lenses, rather than for binoculars.

In Berkshire County alone, 1650 species of flowering plants have been found — more species than most birders traveling the world will see in a lifetime. To learn the name of a plant is to make a friend. Plants do not sprout from the ground with names attached to them, of course. Plant names are of human design: reference points, useful tools for distinguishing one entity from another. The best way to get to know a plant is to learn its name. Aside from having someone else tell you that name, the most pleasurable way to get to know the plants around you and their names is with a field guide.

If you visit or live in the Berkshire and Taconic hills, you will find Joseph Strauch Jr.'s *Wildflowers of the Berkshire & Taconic Hills* to be a welcome companion. Here you will find user-friendly descriptions and striking photographs of what the author has chosen as the "most common, conspicuous, and colorful herbaceous species of flowering plants that occur in the Berkshires."

Botanical nerds like me rely on technical keys and stiff botanic prose to nail down an identification of a plant unknown to us. Strauch has provided a visual guide based on flower color that is easy to use without the knowledge of technical jargon. This is a book to be enjoyed by the nonbotanist who wishes to garner more enjoyment out of his or her surroundings.

This is the kind of book I wish I had had for my childhood locality when I first became interested in plants. It contains what I then yearned to discover about plants — how to identify them, where to find them, when they bloom, and how we have used them. The accounts of human relationships with plants include their edibility and their historical and modern medicinal uses — the "personality profiles" that hook you into learning more. Here you will find all of that, woven into prose that could be created only by one who knows wildflowers as a pursuit of passion.

The Berkshires are synonymous with beauty. Amid

the broad river valleys, rolling farm country, and the sheltering Berkshire hills are cliffs and granite outcrops, pond and lake edges, innumerable streams, bogs, marshes, fens, and fields, adorned with a mosaic of wildflowers to delight the senses and challenge the mind. With this book as your guide, wildflowers certainly will be your friends for many moments of pleasant wandering, and might well become your lifelong passion. Get to know them, and you will get to know yourself.

Steven Foster
December 1994
Fayetteville, Arkansas

INTRODUCTION

Although a wildflower is beautiful even if the observer has no idea of its name, knowing the name of a flower helps link it to other human knowledge and experience. A name allows you to communicate with others about your observation and arouses their interest. Note the difference in the response you get by telling someone you saw a "funny-shaped yellow flower" in the woods versus saying you saw a yellow lady's slipper. A name gives you entree into the natural and human history of the place where the flower occurs. It lets you discover why that kind of flower grows there, why there are so many or so few of them, how they got there, what their role in the ecology of the site is, how the site differs from other places in the Berkshires, whether the plant is useful to humans, how people might have used it in the past, whether it is edible, whether you can grow it in your yard, and where you can get plants. Not all flowers are beautiful, but they are all interesting.

About 1650 species of flowering plants have been recorded from Berkshire County, one of the largest concentrations of species for a comparable area in the Northeast. This diversity of plants reflects the diversity of habitats that can be found here. In the Berkshires, you will find narrow and broad river valleys, rolling countryside, and mountainous terrain. The area's altitude ranges from 577 feet, where the Hoosic River enters Vermont, to 3491 feet, at the top of Mount Greylock. Seven river systems are found here: Bash Bish, Deerfield, Farmington, Housatonic, Hoosic, Kinderhook, and Westfield — and nearly 200 lakes and ponds, including Berry Pond in Pittsfield State Forest, which is the highest natural water body in Massachusetts.

The natural vegetation is mainly eastern deciduous forest but includes representatives of the boreal forest, especially on Mount Greylock, and the Atlantic coastal plain. Plant communities include several kinds of forests and woodlands, both coniferous and deciduous; rocky areas and cliffs; a great variety of wet habitats such as streams and rivers, lakes and ponds, swamps, marshes, bogs, and fens; and those on human-created habitats such as pastures, old fields, roadsides, and power lines. Depending on the underlying rocks, soils may be acidic or alkaline, adding another element of complexity to the mosaic of sites in which different plants may be found.

It is beyond the scope of this guide to cover all the wildflowers that occur in the Berkshires; rather the book is designed to be an introduction for residents and visitors with an interest in discovering more about the wildflowers of this interesting area. Included are photographs and descriptions of 167 of the most common, conspicuous, and colorful herbaceous species of flowering plants that occur in the Berkshires. I have tried to include the species that you are most likely to encounter as you explore the area. Additional similar species are mentioned in the text.

Most of the species accounts give information about the biology or human use of the plant, often including past and current medicinal uses. *Neither the author nor the publisher recommends the use of any plant for medical treatment or vouches for the efficacy or safety of such use.* Information on edibility comes from published sources, but no part of any plant should be ingested unless the person doing so is certain of the plant's identity and safety.

I hope that this book adds to your enjoyment of the Berkshires. In addition, I hope that it helps you appreciate the wonders of the natural world both here and elsewhere and that you will be inspired to help preserve a valuable heritage, much of which we are so close to losing forever.

ACKNOWLEDGMENTS

I could not have written this book with out the help of many other people. I owe a debt to the many botanists who have explored the Northeast and studied its flora since earliest colonial times. A special thanks is due Pamela Weatherbee, whose "Flora of Berkshire County" was indispensable in guiding my field work.

Many people, including naturalists, horticulturists, and property owners, helped me find plants to photograph and let me wander on property they owned or managed. They include Don Reid, The Trustees of Reservations; René Laubach and Marilyn Flor, Massachusetts Audubon Society; Paul Martin Brown; Gertrude Burdsall; Duke Douillet; Alvah Sanborn; Elmer Mellen; Sherry Macdonald; Lucia Saradoff; David Burdick; Dennis Mareb; Mark and Mary Mantuani; Anne Braman; Elizabeth Toffey; Andy Smith; Will Ketchum; Gretchen Finley; and Bill Niering.

I thank Jean Rousseau and Philip Rich of Berkshire House Publishers for their encouragement and efforts in producing this volume, and Sarah Novak for her expert editing.

Betsy Strauch advised me on the uses of plants and tightened up my original sprawling prose.

HOW TO USE THIS BOOK

The species covered in this book are arranged by flower color and by bloom season within a color. The color categories used are

> white to cream,
> yellow to orange,
> pink to red,
> purple to blue,
> green to brown.

Assigning a species to a color category can be rather arbitrary, especially for flowers that shade from pink to purple. Occasionally a species that usually has white flowers will have pink ones. Albino (white) flowers appear sporadically in many species. Often flower color changes with age. Sometimes the light affects how a color is perceived. If you can't find a species in one category, try another that is close to it. Bloom periods are approximate and may vary by a week or two depending on local weather patterns. In general, widespread species bloom earlier in the southern part of our area than in the northern part and bloom earlier at lower elevations than at higher ones. Many of the woodland species bloom before the trees leaf out in the spring and disappear by midsummer.

The numbers and arrangements of the parts of a plant are important for identification. The number of petals (or what appear to be petals), whether the flowers are solitary or clustered, the arrangement and the shape of the leaves, and the plant's habit are all clues to identification. The diagrams on pp. xx and xxi illustrate the diagnostic features used in this guide.

The characteristics of a species often vary within a population. It is a good idea to look at several plants to determine the most common condition for a given feature.

I recommend that you spend some time looking at the pictures and reading some of the species accounts to familiarize yourself with flower types before trying to make identifications. This will also give you an idea of which flowers are likely to occur at a given time of year and where you might find them. (The photographs of the plants are keyed to the text by the plate number given at the top right-hand corner of each description.)

If after comparing a flower to the photographs and text you come to a dead end, you might have one of the approximately 1500 species in the Berkshires that are not covered by this book. In that case, you may want to consult a more comprehensive field guide (see References, pp. 119–20). Be aware, however, that many species either are not covered in any field guide or require technical manuals and/or herbaria (collections of dried specimens) for correct identification.

Many of the locations where wildflowers are to be found are in sanctuaries, where picking flowers is strictly prohibited. The same rule applies to private property unless you have the owner's permission to pick flowers. I have provided sufficient information to identify the wildflowers covered in this book without damaging them in any way. Although it may be easier to get a closer look at a plant by picking off a piece or pulling it up, please don't unless you are at a site where the plant is not protected and you are certain that destroying one individual will not be detrimental to the local population. Never disturb a plant if fewer than a dozen individuals are in the immediate area. Beyond this, use your best judgment but consider, if you are on a popular trail, what would happen if everyone who passed by picked just one plant. Please be considerate of the environment and others who also enjoy it.

PLANT PARTS AND ARRANGEMENTS

Figure 1. The parts of a typical flower.

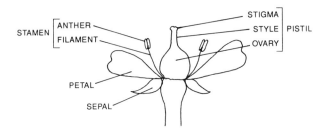

Figure 2. Common types of inflorescences (flower clusters) and leaf arrangements.

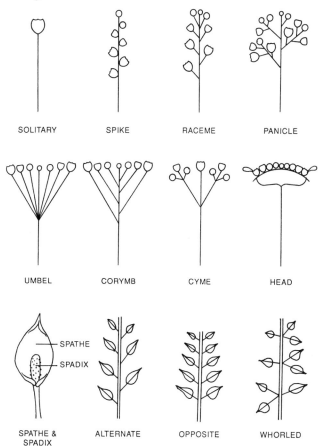

SOLITARY   SPIKE   RACEME   PANICLE

UMBEL   CORYMB   CYME   HEAD

SPATHE
SPADIX

SPATHE &   ALTERNATE   OPPOSITE   WHORLED
SPADIX

AREA COVERED IN THIS BOOK

The Berkshires consist of Berkshire County, Massachusetts, as well as the extension of the Berkshire Hills (Berkshire Plateau and Hoosac Range) to the east and the Taconic Range west into New York State and south into Connecticut as shown in the accompanying map. Most of the species covered, however, have much larger ranges and can be found throughout the northeastern United States.

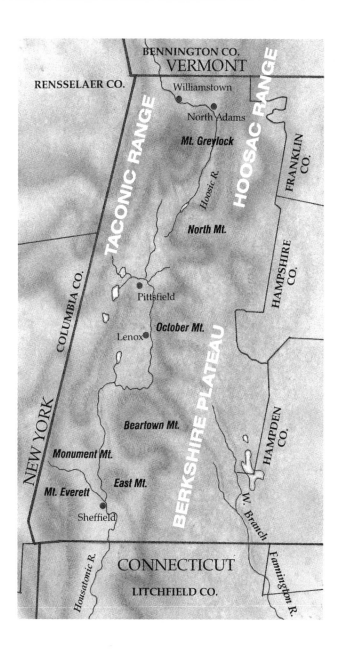

GLOSSARY

anther: The part of the stamen that bears the pollen.

axil: The upper angle where the leaf joins the stem.

basal: At the base of the stem or other structure.

bract: A small or modified leaf found at the base of a flower, flower head, or leaf petiole.

calyx: The outer circle of flower parts; the sepals collectively.

compound leaf: A leaf divided into two or more leaflets.

compound umbel: An umbel of umbels.

cordate: Heart shaped, usually referring to the base of a leaf.

corolla: The inner circle of flower parts; the petals collectively.

corymb: A flat-topped raceme.

cyme: A flower cluster in which the terminal flower blooms first.

disk flower: Small tubular flowers found in the heads of the aster family. They may be the only type present, as in a thistle, or be surrounded with ray flowers, as in a daisy.

filament: The stalk of a stamen.

head: A tight cluster of stemless or nearly stemless flowers as found in the aster family.

lanceolate: Referring to a leaf or other structure that is longer than wide and tapering at one end.

leaflet: The smallest leaflike part of a compound leaf.

mycorrhizal: Referring to a symbiotic relationship of a fungus with the roots of a plant.

node: The point on a stem at which a leaf is attached.

ovate: Referring to a leaf or other structure that is egg shaped with the wider end toward the base.

palmate: With parts radiating from a common point like fingers on a hand.

panicle: A branched raceme.

petal: A segment of the corolla.

petiole: A leaf stalk.

pinnate: With parts, usually leaflets of a leaf, radiating from a common stalk; arranged like barbs on a feather. A leaf is said to be compound pinnate if the stalk is branched.

pistil: The female organ of a flower, consisting of a stigma and style.

raceme: An unbranched, elongate flower cluster in which the flowers are stalked and the lower flowers open first.

ray flower: A flower with a strap-shaped petal found in the heads of the aster family. They may be the only type of flower present, as in a dandelion, or ring the edge of a group of ray flowers, as in a sunflower.

receptacle: The basal part of a flower or flower head.

recurved: Bent backward

rhizome: A creeping underground stem.

rosette: A circular cluster of parts, such as leaves at the base of a stem.

sepal: A segment of the calyx, usually green, but sometimes colored.

sessile: Directly attached without a stalk.

sheath: An organ surrounding another organ, such as a leaf base surrounding a stem.

spadix: A dense spike of tiny flowers on a fleshy axis.

spathe: A large bract surrounding or enclosing a spadix.

spike: An elongated flower cluster in which the flowers are stalkless or nearly so.

stamen: The male organ of a flower, consisting of a filament and an anther.

stigma: The tip of the pistil that receives the pollen; it is usually divided or knobby.

style: The stalk of the pistil.

tendril: A slender, coiling structure often used for climbing and support.

tepal: A segment of a flower in which the sepals and petals are indistinguishable.

umbel: A flower cluster in which all of the flower stalks radiate from the same point like the spokes of an inverted umbrella.

whorl: A cluster of three or more parts radiating from the same point.

WHERE TO FIND WILDFLOWERS

You don't have to visit a wilderness to find wildflowers; they occur almost everywhere. Most garden weeds are wildflowers as is much of the vegetation on roadsides and around parking lots and along paths and trails. The saying that nature abhors a vacuum is certainly true of wildflowers: one or another of them will find every bare piece of ground. You'll find them at cultural sites. For example, the grounds at Tanglewood probably support more than 100 species of wildflowers; look for them before or after a concert or while just strolling the grounds. If you want to find a large variety of wildflowers, however, you'll have to visit different sites because species differ in their environmental requirements and many of them cannot survive in disturbed habitats. The kinds you're likely to find in disturbed areas are pioneers, which are quick to find a new opening. These species tend to form many seeds, which often have special structures to help them get around — little tufts of fluff that catch the wind or little hooks that latch onto the fur of passing mammals. These are often alien species that have been introduced by humans. When white settlers arrived in North America, the Northeast was heavily wooded, with little habitat for open-country species. As the woods were cleared, species introduced from Europe, which were well adapted to open country, rapidly took hold and spread. To find native species, you will have to visit native habitats such as woods and natural wetlands.

Fortunately, there are many such areas within easy driving distance. Good sources of information include René Laubach's *A Guide to Natural Places in the Berkshire Hills* and Lauren R. Stevens's *Hikes and Walks in the Berkshire Hills*. Additional guides, especially for the mountains, can be found in bookstores and shops that cater to hikers. If you'd like to hunt wildflowers with local naturalists, check out the many nature hikes and workshops offered by the Massachusetts Audubon Society (413-637-0320) at their Pleasant Valley and Canoe Meadows sanctuaries, The Trustees of Reservations (413-298-3239) at Bartholomew's Cobble, and the Appalachian Mountain Club (413-684-3900). Maps and information for state parks and forests can be obtained at the Massachusetts Department of Environmental Management Regional Headquarters and Visitor Center, 740 South St., Pittsfield (413-442-8928).

Wildflowers

White to Cream Flowers

Alliaria petiolata   April   Plate **2A**
Garlic Mustard   Mustard Family
    In early spring, you may find a plant with dense terminal clusters of 1/3-inch, 4-petaled white flowers. If the foliage smells like garlic when bruised, you have found garlic mustard. The alternate, toothed leaves are triangular with a heart-shaped base, and may be up to 4 inches long. The stem is smooth, and the plant may reach 4 feet in height.
    Garlic mustard was introduced from Europe and can be found in most open habitats in the Berkshires.
    The leaves can be used to flavor salads or mild cooked greens. In 19th century England, this plant was often the only condiment available to poor people for their bread and fish, and was known as Sauce Alone. If eaten by cows, it gives their milk an off-flavor.

Sanguinaria canadensis   April   Plate **1**
Bloodroot, Red Puccoon   Poppy Family
    Spring has truly arrived when bloodroot blooms. Look for its simple 8-petaled flower on a stalk up to 1 foot tall sheathed by the unopened leaf. The flowers last only a day or two and are closed at night or in dim light. The flowers are usually gone by the time the single palmate leaf with 5 to 9 lobes is fully open. The seeds are dispersed by ants, which are attracted to a fleshy appendage on the seed.

Bloodroot has a long and continuing history of medicinal uses. The bright red juice of the root was used by American Indians as a dye and love potion as well as to treat cancer. It was formerly used as a cough medicine and is currently used in toothpaste and mouthwash to inhibit plaque formation. The juice is potentially poisonous; it contains a corrosive substance that is currently used to treat skin cancers.

Bloodroot is found in moist woods but may persist after the land is cleared. Look for it at Pleasant Valley Sanctuary, at Bartholomew's Cobble, and in Kennedy Park. The species is widely cultivated, and a double form is available.

Cardamine (Dentaria) diphylla   April–May   Plate **2B**
Two-leaved Toothwort,
Pepper Root   Mustard Family

The toothworts are among the earliest of spring flowers. They can be recognized by their 4-petaled white flowers. The flowers are about 3/4 inch wide and occur in terminal clusters. Two-leaved toothwort has 2 nearly opposite leaves on the flowering stem and a group of basal leaves. The leaves, which may reach 5 inches in length, are 3-parted with ovate, toothed leaflets. The stems are unbranched and up to 14 inches tall.

The rhizomes may be eaten fresh in salads or ground in vinegar and used like horseradish. Some American Indians chewed the roots for colds. The roots were also a folk remedy for toothache.

Toothworts may be found in moist woods. Look for them on Mount Greylock, at Pleasant Valley Sanctuary, and at Bartholomew's Cobble.

Cut-leaved toothwort, *C. concatenata (laciniata)*, will

also be found in similar locations in the Berkshires. It can be distinguished from two-leaved toothwort by a whorl of 3 leaves on the flowering stem and a lack of basal leaves at flowering time. The leaves are divided into 5 or more deeply toothed, lanceolate leaflets. Cut-leaved toothwort tends to bloom about a week earlier than two-leaved toothwort.

Dicentra cucullaria   April–May   Plate **2C**
Dutchman's Breeches, Blue Staggers   Poppy Family
    In April, watch for 10-inch mounds of feathery bluish green foliage under dangling 2-spurred white flowers that resemble upside-down pantaloons. The flowers are about 1/2 to 3/4 inch long and occur in 1-sided clusters of 4 to 8 flowers on a thin leafless stem. The leaves are basal, pinnately divided into 5 dissected segments. By midsummer, the plants have completed their annual cycle and are dormant.
    The plant was once used in a poultice as a folk remedy for skin ailments. The leaves and tubers contain toxic alkaloids; livestock eating them may become uncoordinated in a condition known as staggers.
    Dutchman's breeches are found in rich, moist woods and on rocky ledges. They are widespread in the Berkshires, occurring on Mount Greylock, at Pleasant Valley Sanctuary, and Bartholomew's Cobble along the Ledges Trail. A similar species, *D. canadensis*, squirrel corn, is found in the northern part of our area. It is distinguished from Dutchman's breeches by its heart-shaped flowers.

Saxifraga virginiensis   April–May   Plate **2D**
Early Saxifrage   Saxifrage Family
    Watch for a small plant (about 4 inches tall) with
basal leaves and a leafless, sticky, hairy flower stalk
holding a branching cluster of small 5-petaled white
flowers. The leaves are oval with toothed edges and
often are purple on the underside. After flowering, the
plant may grow to 16 inches tall.
    Early saxifrage is easily found on rocky ledges and
cliffs on Mount Greylock and at Bartholomew's Cobble.

Fragaria vesca   April–June   Plate **2E**
Wood Strawberry   Rose Family
    Wood strawberries can be recognized by their 5-pet-
aled white flowers with many stamens and by their 3-
parted leaflets. The 1/2-inch flowers occur singly or in
clusters of as many as 9 on leafless stalks. The evergreen
leaves are basal, and the toothed leaflets may be up to 1
1/2 inches long. The plant may reach 6 inches in height
with flowers and fruit held above the leaves. The fruit
tends to be cone-shaped.
    The fruit is one of nature's treats, and the leaves may
be used to brew a pleasant tea. Some American Indians
used a tea brewed from the roots to treat stomach ailments and jaundice. The fruit is eaten by many species
of birds and is an important part of the diet of box
turtles.
    Watch for wood strawberries in open woods, fields,
and along roadsides throughout the Berkshires.
    The wild strawberry, *F. virginiana*, is also commonly
found in fields. Features that distinguish it from the
wood strawberry include larger flowers (up to 1 inch
wide), leaves and flowering stalk about the same height,

roundish fruit, and the terminal tooth of the leaflets shorter than the 2 adjoining teeth.

Mitella diphylla   April–June   Plate **2F**
Miterwort, Bishop's Cap,
Coolwort   Saxifrage Family
    Miterwort is a delicate plant with a 6-inch spike of 5 to 20 tiny, 1/4 inch white flowers. These intricate flowers have 5 finely divided petals and resemble snowflakes. The plant has a basal cluster of long-stalked lobed leaves with heart-shaped bases. The flowering stalk has 2 opposite, sessile, 3-lobed leaves. The seed capsule resembles a bishop's miter. A less common species, naked miterwort, *M. nuda*, is smaller and has a leafless flowering stem.
    Miterwort can be found in moist woods, often growing on rocks. Look for it on Mount Greylock, at Pleasant Valley Sanctuary, at Bartholomew's Cobble, in Kennedy Park, and at Notchview Reservation.

Actaea alba   May   Plate **3A**
White Baneberry, Doll's Eyes   Buttercup Family
    Little white bottle brushes found in the woods in May are likely to be a flowers of a species of baneberry. Those of white baneberry are about 1/4 inch wide with long stamens that cause the individual flowers to appear globular. The flowers occur in cylindrical racemes 1 to 2 inches wide and 2 to 4 inches long that are held above the foliage. The plant is erect, growing to 2 1/2 feet tall with leaves that are 2 or 3 times divided into ovate to lanceolate toothed leaflets up to 4 inches long. The fruit, which is present in late summer and fall, is a white berry

about 3/8 inch in diameter with a prominent black dot, giving rise to the common name doll's eyes.

Some American Indians made a tea from the plant that they used to treat the pain of childbirth, other intense pain, and inflammations of the mouth. The plant is poisonous, however. The berries can cause pain and inflammation of the mouth and, if swallowed, increased heart rate, irritation of the digestive tract, and dizziness. The rhizome is a violent purgative and may cause skin blisters.

Both white baneberry and the similar red baneberry, *A. rubra*, are found in rich, moist woods throughout the Berkshires. Red baneberry has more rounded flower racemes and finer flower and fruit stalks than those of white baneberry. The stalks of the latter are about as thick as a pencil lead. Red baneberry has bright red fruit. Occasionally the fruit of white baneberry is a washed-out red, but the plant is easily identified by the thick fruit stalks.

Anemone quinquefolia   May   Plate **3B**
Wood Anemone   Buttercup Family
You'll find wood anemones in woodlands in early spring. The solitary white flowers are about 1 inch wide and consist of 5 petallike sepals; there are no petals. The flowers open only in bright light, closing at night and on cloudy days. Leaves occur as a basal rosette and as a whorl of 3 just below the flowers. Individual leaves have long stalks and are palmately divided into 3 to 5 sharp-toothed segments, each about 1 1/4 inches long. The stems are smooth, and the plant may be up to 8 inches tall.

Wood anemones are found in moist areas in open woods, clearings, and woodland borders.

Anemones are poisonous and can cause irritation

of the skin and mucous membranes. Wood anemone is sometimes cultivated in woodland gardens.

Wood anemones can be found along the Spero Trail at Bartholomew's Cobble.

Anthriscus sylvestris   May   Plate **3C**
Wild Chervil   Parsley (Carrot) Family
Wild chervil forms billowy clouds of white along Berkshire roadways in the spring. The tiny white flowers occur in large compound umbels (with 6 to 10 primary rays) in leaf axils or terminally. The alternate leaves are twice compound with segments up to 2 inches long. The plant may reach 3 feet tall.

The species has been introduced from Europe and is found in damp areas along roadsides and field borders.

The plant can be used like chervil (*A. cerefolium*) or eaten as a potherb; however, it can cause photodermatitis. There are several poisonous plants in this family that occur in similar habitats in the Berkshires that might be mistaken for wild chervil.

Wild chervil is especially abundant along Rte. 183 in Stockbridge and Lenox.

Aralia nudicaulis   May   Plate **3D**
Wild Sarsaparilla   Ginseng Family
The most obvious feature of wild sarsaparilla is the large 3-parted leaf which is about 18 inches tall and nearly conceals the leafless flowering stalk. The greenish white flowers in 3 globular clusters have 5 tiny petals and long stamens. Wild sarsaparilla is common throughout wooded areas. The new shoots are shiny and purplish and resemble those of poison ivy

(*Toxicodendron radicans*). The fruit is a blue black berry.

The aromatic rhizome can be used as tea. It has also been used as a substitute for true sarsaparilla (*Smilax officinalis*) to flavor root beer. American Indians used it for a cough medicine, and it was a common ingredient in 19th-century patent medicines.

Wild sarsaparilla is a common plant on Mount Greylock, in Kennedy Park, at Pleasant Valley Sanctuary, and at Bartholomew's Cobble.

Trillium undulatum   May   Plate **3E**
Painted Trillium   Lily Family
The 3 white petals with a deep red V at their base make painted trillium unmistakable. The flower is about 2 1/2 inches wide and ill-smelling. The 3 leaves, in a whorl just below the flower, may be as much as 5 inches long and have slender, pointed tips. The entire plant may be 1 1/2 feet tall.

Painted trillium has been used in ways similar to red trillium, *T. erectum* (see p. 68).

Watch for painted trillium in moist woods, often under conifers. It occurs on Mount Greylock, at Pleasant Valley Sanctuary, and at Notchview Reservation.

Antennaria neglecta   May–June   Plate **3F**
Pussytoes, Ladies' Tobacco   Aster Family
In open dry areas such as lawns and fields, you will frequently find mats of silvery or woolly leaves, up to 2 inches long, in little rosettes. In May and June, the rosettes produce stalks to about 15 inches tall topped by clusters of bristly flower heads. The individual heads, consisting entirely of disk flowers mixed with many

silky hairs, are thought to resemble cat's toes. Plants are either male or female. Those with pinkish heads are pistillate (male) whereas those with white ones are staminate (female).

The plant was little used in folk remedies, but dried plants are sometimes used as a moth repellent. The flower stalks can be used in dried flower arrangements. Grouse, deer, and hares often eat the foliage. This and related species are commonly grown in rock gardens, and pink and red varieties are available.

A second species, plantain-leaved pussytoes, *A. plantaginifolia*, is also found in the Berkshires. It tends to have larger basal leaves (to 3 inches long) which have 3 major veins as compared to 1 in *A. neglecta*.

Cornus canadensis   May–June   Plate **4A**
Bunchberry, Dwarf Cornel   Dogwood Family

Bunchberry is an herbaceous plant up to 10 inches tall which spreads by rhizomes to form large mats. If you are familiar with flowering dogwood (*Cornus florida*) you will easily recognize bunchberry, which looks as though flowers and foliage of the tree had been spread over the ground. Each stalk bears a whorl of 4 to 6 oval pointed leaves with parallel veins. What appears at first glance to be the flower is actually 4 large white bracts which surround a small cluster of inconspicuous greenish flowers. In late summer and fall, look for bunches of bright red berries; they are edible but nearly tasteless.

Bunchberry is often used as an ornamental plant. It is fairly easy to grow from seed, but usually doesn't flower well in areas warmer than the Berkshires.

This species occurs in cool, shady wooded areas.

You'll easily find it along the trails on Mount Greylock, on October Mountain, and at Notchview Reservation.

Smilacina racemosa   May–June   Plate **4B**
False Solomon's Seal, False Spikenard   Lily Family
     A tall, arching plant with a feathery, pyramidal, terminal panicle of tiny white flowers may be false Solomon's seal. The flowers are 6-parted, and oblong leaves up to 6 inches long have pointed tips and parallel veins arranged alternately in 2 rows on the zigzagging stem. The plant is usually about 3 feet tall. The fruit is a bright red berry in loose bunches. Seeds are produced without fertilization. (See also Solomon's seal, *Polygonatum biflorum*, p. 40.)
     The young shoots can be used in salads or cooked like asparagus. The berries are eaten by ruffed grouse, thrushes, other birds, and small mammals. Berries can be eaten as a trail snack, but with moderation since they are cathartic.
     False Solomon's seal is common in moist woods. Look for it in Kennedy Park, at Pleasant Valley Sanctuary, on Mount Greylock, and at Bartholomew's Cobble.

Tiarella cordifolia   May–June   Plate **4C**
Foamflower, False Miterwort   Saxifrage Family
     Foamflower is well named since the tiny white flowers with their long stamens give the short dense terminal raceme a distinctly fuzzy appearance. The 5-petaled flowers occur on a leafless stem. The basal leaves have long stalks and are hairy with shallow lobes somewhat resembling those of maple leaves.
     American Indians used foamflower to make a tea to

treat mouth and eye ailments, possibly because of its high tannin content.

Watch for large colonies of foamflower in moist woods on Mount Greylock, on Savoy Mountain, at Pleasant Valley Sanctuary, at Bartholomew's Cobble, and in Kennedy Park. The species is widely cultivated.

Trientalis borealis   May–June   Plate **4D**
Starflower   Primrose Family

A small white woodland flower with 7 petals is probably starflower. The flowers are about 2/3 inch wide, solitary, and are held on thin stalks over a single whorl of 5 to 9 shiny lanceolate leaves. The plant grows to about 10 inches tall.

Look for starflower in moist woods and in bogs on October Mountain, on Mount Greylock, in Kennedy Park, at Pleasant Valley Sanctuary, and at Bartholomew's Cobble. Starflower is a favorite ground cover for rock gardens.

Viola canadensis   May–June   Plate **4E**
Canada Violet, Tall White Violet   Violet Family

A tall white violet with a yellow throat and the back of the petals tinged purple is probably this species. The flowers occur on stems in the axils of the alternate stem leaves. The basal leaves are long-stalked and heart shaped. The plant may reach 16 inches in height. Canada violet, like many other species of violet, produces two kinds of flowers: the regular ones we notice, and unopening, self-pollinating ones that also produce seeds. The seeds are dispersed by ants.

The leaves and flowers of violets are a good source

of vitamin C and traditionally have been used as a trail snack, in salads, jelly, and jams, and candied. Violets have a long history of medicinal use, but their effects were mild at best. American Indians made a tea from the roots to treat bladder pain.

Watch for Canada violet in moist woods. It is quite common on Mount Greylock. The species is widely cultivated, and dwarf varieties and those with pure white flowers are available.

Twenty-three species of violets have been recorded in the Berkshires. They can be told apart on the basis of their flower color and leaf arrangement and shape. However, because of the variability of leaf shape, other characteristics beyond the scope of this book are often necessary for positive identification.

Seven species have white flowers. Of these, Canada violet is the only species with stem leaves; the other six have only basal leaves and are differentiated on the basis of leaf shape. Lance-leaf violet, *V. lanceolata*, has lance-shaped leaves; kidney-leaved violet, *V. renifolia*, has kidney-shaped leaves; and primrose violet, *V. primulifolia*, has oblong leaves with long petioles. The other three species with white flowers have heart-shaped leaves: large-leaf violet, *V. incognita*, has downy stalks; sweet white violet, *V. blanda*, has pointed leaves; and smooth white violet, *V. macloskeyi*, has blunt leaves. There is considerable overlap in the leaf shape of the last two species.

Three species have yellow flowers. Only early yellow violet, *V. rotundifolia*, has only basal leaves. *Viola pubescens* in the past has been divided into two species, downy yellow violet and smooth yellow violet, but these are now considered to be varieties of a single species. They have bright yellow flowers and are common and widely distributed. Wild pansy, *V. arvensis*, is a European species which has escaped from gardens. It has pale yellow flowers which often have purple tips, and is uncommon here.

Thirteen species have blue to purple flowers. The only species that have stem leaves are long-spurred violet, *V. rostrata*, in which the flower has an obvious spur about 1/2 inch long, and dog violet, *V. conspersa*, in which the flower has a spur about 1/4 inch long.

The 11 blue-flowered species with only basal leaves are tricky to tell apart. Early blue violet, *V. palmata*, and three-lobed violet, *V. triloba*, both have lobed leaves. Those of early blue violet tend to have more and narrower lobes, but there is considerable overlap, and some authors consider them to be the same species. Fringed violet, *V. fimbriatula*, and arrow-leaved violet, *V. sagittata*, have lance-shaped leaves, with those of arrow-leaved violet being lobed at the base; again there is considerable overlap, and some consider them to be a variable species. The other seven species have heart-shaped leaves, and separation of them is beyond the scope of this book.

Calla palustris   June   Plate **4F**
Wild Calla   Arum Family
This species is found in areas with wet soils, such as bogs, marshes, or the borders of ponds. Look for a plant about 12 inches tall with a sharply pointed white hood (spathe) about 2 inches long enclosing a yellowish cylinder (spadix) about 1 inch tall. The actual flowers are yellow and very tiny. The leaves grow from the base of the plant and are shiny green and heart shaped with long petioles. The flowers develop into clusters of red berries.

In Lapland, the rhizomes are dried and ground into flour to make bread. Some American Indians made a tea from the dried rhizomes to treat flu. Attempting to eat any part of the fresh plant produces a painful burning sensation because it contains crystals of calcium oxalate.

Wild calla can be found in wet areas on October Mountain.

Heracleum lanatum   June   Plate **5A**
Cow Parsnip, Masterwort   Parsley (Carrot) Family

A tall (to 10 feet), robust plant found in rich, moist soils on floodplains and shorelines may be this species. The small white flowers occur in flat-topped umbels up to 8 inches wide. The flowers have 5 petals, some of which are longer and deeply notched. The leaves, arranged alternately on the stem, are about 2 feet long and divided into 3 leaflets, each of which resembles a maple leaf. The bases of the petioles are inflated and sheathe the stem. The somewhat similar purple-stem angelica, *Angelica atropurpurea* (p.25), has inflated leaf bases but spherical flower clusters. The main stem is thick, hollow, ridged, and covered with woolly hairs.

Wild food enthusiasts eat the stems and roots. American Indians used cow parsnip to treat a variety of ailments, and they used the ashes of burnt leaves as a salt substitute. This species and related ones may cause contact dermatitis, and the sap may cause blisters. There are so many dangerous but similar-looking plants in this family that they should never be handled or eaten unless their identity is certain. On the other hand, they can be safely studied and admired at a short distance.

Maianthemum canadense   June   Plate **5B**
Canada Mayflower,
False Lily-of-the-Valley   Lily Family

Canada mayflower is a small plant, usually about 6 inches tall, with a 1-inch terminal raceme of many tiny white flowers. The fragrant flowers have 4 tepals, a good feature for identification. Two or 3 pointed unstalked leaves with heart-shaped bases are arranged alternately on the smooth, zigzagging stem. The fruit is a small berry which at first is white with dark spots and later bright red. These are often eaten by ruffed grouse and small mammals. The similar three-lobed Solomon's seal, *Smilacina trifolia*, has 6-petaled flowers and lanceolate leaves, and is found only in wet areas.

Canada mayflower berries are edible but purgative, and thus should only be eaten in small amounts. Some American Indians wore the root as a good-luck charm.

This species is common in moist woods and often forms large colonies. Look for them on Mount Greylock, at Canoe Meadows Sanctuary, at Pleasant Valley Sanctuary, in Kennedy Park, and on October Mountain.

Apocynum cannabinum   June–July   Plate **5C**
Indian Hemp   Dogbane Family

A shrublike plant with greenish white 1/4-inch flowers may be Indian hemp. The flowers are bell-like with 5 pointed lobes and occur in terminal clusters. The opposite leaves are ovate to elliptical with a pointed tip and a distinct stalk. They may reach 5 inches long. The branched stems are erect and may reach 3 1/2 feet tall. The plant has milky juice.

American Indians used the stem fibers to make ropes and thread, and entire stems for baskets and mats. Colonists traded bread for Indian hemp ropes. The plant is poisonous and has been used as a fish poison; the milky juice is a folk remedy for venereal warts.

Watch for Indian hemp in damp areas along roads and water bodies. It occurs around the edges of Mill Pond in South Egremont and at Bartholomew's Cobble.

Geum canadense   June–July   Plate **5D**
White Avens   Rose Family

White avens is a rather unshowy plant with 1/2-inch, 5-petaled white flowers. The petals and sepals are about the same length. The stamens are numerous and the receptacle bristly. The leaves are alternate, the upper ones simple and the lower ones compound with 3 toothed terminal leaflets. The branched stems are smooth to slightly hairy and may reach 3 1/2 feet tall.

This species is common in woods and along shady roadsides. You can find it at Pleasant Valley Sanctuary and Bartholomew's Cobble.

The similar rough avens, *G. laciniatum*, has petals shorter than the sepals and hairy stems.

Leucanthemum vulgare   June–July   Plate **5E**
Oxeye Daisy   Aster Family

This is the white daisy that grows along roads and in fields and meadows. The 2-inch flower heads have white ray flowers and yellow disk flowers. Plants grow to about 2 1/2 feet and have coarsely toothed alternate leaves. The number of ray flowers varies from 15 to 35, and this characteristic has been used as a class exercise to illustrate the statistics of biological variation.

The plant is edible, but the flavor appeals to few

people. When eaten by dairy cattle it gives an off-flavor to milk. The plant has been declared an noxious weed in several states became of this.

A native of Europe, oxeye daisy is now found through the Northeast and cultivated as an ornamental. Numerous cultivars are available.

Melilotus alba   June–July   Plate **5F**
White Sweet Clover, White Melilot   Pea Family

Large, airy plants covered with white blossoms in midsummer may be this species. The 1/4-inch white flowers are pealike and occur in long axillary clusters to 8 inches. The alternate leaves are compound with 3 1-inch leaflets. The smooth stems are branched and may be up to 8 feet tall. The plant is fragrant when dried or crushed.

The spring leaves may be eaten raw or cooked; tea brewed from the flowers and leaves has a vanilla flavor. In England, the plant is used to make melilot plasters for wounds and sores.

This species is often planted as a forage crop or for green manure to improve soil fertility. Moldy hay of sweet clover can cause hemorrhaging in livestock. An introduction from Europe, white sweet clover is commonly found in fields, along roadsides, and in waste areas. Yellow sweet clover, *M. officinalis*, is similar but has yellow flowers.

Stellaria aquatica   June–July   Plate **6A**
Giant Chickweed, Stitchwort   Pink Family

Chickweeds and stitchworts are weak, sprawly plants with small 5-petaled white flowers that are so deeply cleft that at first glance they appear to be 10-petaled. They are separated by botanists into two genera, *Cerastium* and *Stellaria*, on the basis of differences in their fruit; they may also be divided by their leaf width into the wider-leaved chickweeds and the narrower-leaved stitchworts. The 1/2-inch flowers of giant chickweed are large for the group. They occur in terminal clusters on the ends of long stalks arising from the upper leaf axils. The leaves are opposite, oval with pointed tips, sessile, and may reach 3 1/2 inches long. The branched stems, covered with fine hairs, are often prostrate.

This species was introduced from Europe. Watch for it in wet areas such as the edges of marshes, roadside ditches, and meadows. There is a good stand of it behind Bascom Lodge on Mount Greylock.

Thalictrum pubescens   June–July   Plate **6B**
Tall Meadow Rue   Buttercup Family
Tall meadow rue is a tall, feathery plant. It has 1/3-inch white flowers with no petals in large, loose, branching, plumelike clusters. The bluish green leaves are alternate, more than once ternately divided into 1-inch leaflets with 3 lobes. The stems are smooth to slightly hairy and may reach 8 feet tall.

This is a common species throughout the Berkshires in moist areas, roadside ditches, and meadows. Look for it at Savoy State Forest, Pleasant Valley Sanctuary, and Bartholomew's Cobble.

Valeriana officinalis   June–July   Plate **6C**
Common Valerian,
Garden Heliotrope   Valerian Family

In midsummer, common valerian will appear as tall roadside plants with clusters of pinkish white flowers. The 1/4-inch flowers are funnel shaped with 5 lobes. The opposite leaves are compound, with 5 to 25 lance-shaped leaflets that are often toothed. The stem is erect, hairy at the nodes, and may reach 5 feet in height.

Common valerian, introduced from Europe, has been used to treat many ailments. The powdered root was once a treatment for nervous disorders. Modern research has confirmed that teas, tinctures, or extracts act as a central nervous system depressant, antispasmodic, antibacterial, antidiuretic, and liver protective. This plant is used in a leading over-the-counter tranquilizer in Europe but is not approved as a drug in the United States.

Rats and cats are said to be attracted to the plant's scent, and the Pied Piper was said to have carried a valerian root to lure the rats from Hamelin.

Common valerian can be found in moist areas along roadsides and in meadows. A big patch of it grows along the highway at Notchview Reservation, and it occurs at Bartholomew's Cobble.

Achillea millefolium   June–August   Plate **6D**
Yarrow, Milfoil   Aster Family

Yarrow has numerous 1/4-inch-wide flower heads held in flat-topped corymbs on erect stems with fern-like aromatic foliage. The flowers are white or sometimes pinkish. The leaves are gray green, to about 6 inches long, sessile, and arranged alternately. The plant may grow to 3 feet tall.

The fresh plant has been used since ancient times as an astringent to treat wounds and nosebleed. A tea made by boiling the foliage in milk has been used to treat fever by inducing sweating. The leaves were once chewed to relieve toothache. Yarrow was once used in place of hops to flavor beer. However, the plant contains thujone, which in large amounts causes convulsions, and thus is potentially harmful if taken in large or frequent doses.

This species and its hybrids are popular garden plants and are available in many pastel and bright shades of yellow, orange, pink, and red. It is frequently used in dried flower arrangements.

Yarrow can be found throughout the Berkshires in open fields, lawns, along roadsides, and in waste areas. Although the species is native to North America, Berkshire plants appear to be the introduced European subspecies. (They are distinguished by analysis of their chromosomes.)

Chelone glabra   June–August   Plate **6E**
Turtlehead, Balmony   Figwort Family

The flower of this species resembles a turtle with its mouth open. White tinged with pink, and about 1 to 1 1/2 inches long, it has 2 lips with the upper overlapping the lower. The flowers occur in dense terminal spikes. The leaves are smooth, lanceolate, and toothed, and have prominent veins. They are arranged oppositely. The plant may be up to 4 feet tall and is usually branched at the top.

Turtlehead was once used to treat liver disorders, as a laxative, and to worm children. An ointment made from the plant was used to treat hemorrhoids, inflamed breasts, and herpes.

Turtlehead can be found in wet areas, along streams, in ditches, and in woods and meadows. You can find it on Mount Greylock, at Pleasant Valley Sanctuary, and at Bartholomew's Cobble.

Nymphaea odorata   June–August   Plate **6F**
Fragrant Water Lily   Water Lily family
Large, roselike white flowers floating on the water in the Berkshires are likely to be fragrant water lily. The 5-inch-wide flowers have numerous petals with tapering tips. They open in the morning and close in the afternoon. The floating leaves are round and notched at the base, purplish underneath, and may be 10 inches across. The leaf stalks contain large air channels thought to allow oxygen movement to the rhizome which is buried underwater.

The unopened flowers and young leaves may be used as a potherb. The rhizomes and tubers may be prepared like potatoes, but are quite bitter. The cooked seeds may be eaten whole or ground into flour. Pioneers used the tubers for stomach problems and to make a gargle for sore throat. In folk tradition, the root and lemon juice were used to remove freckles.

An American Indian legend says that the water lily was created from a fallen star. The plants are eaten by cranes, muskrats, beaver, porcupines, and moose; ducks eat the seed.

Fragrant water lily is found on ponds, shallow lakes, and slow-moving streams throughout the Berkshires.

Tuberous water lily, *N. tuberosa*, has been introduced into the Berkshires. Its flowers have blunt-tipped petals and little or no fragrance; the leaves are usually green underneath.

Silene vulgaris   June–August   Plate **7A**
Bladder Campion   Pink Family

The swollen calyx of bladder campion is characteristic of several closely related species found in the Berkshires. The 1-inch-wide white flowers of bladder campion
have 5 deeply notched petals that appear to be 10, 3
styles, and 10 protruding stamens. The bladderlike calyx
is prominently veined. The leaves are ovate to lanceolate
and up to 4 inches long. They are opposite and often
clasp the smooth stem. The stem is often branched, erect
or sprawling, and may reach 2 feet in length.

This introduction from Europe may be found along
roadsides, at the edges of fields and meadows, in gardens, and in waste areas.

The young shoots are said to taste like green peas.
Their slightly bitter taste is due to saponin, which is
poisonous in large quantities.

Similar species found in the Berkshires include
sleepy catchfly, *S. antirrhina*, the flowers of which are
only about 1/8 inch wide; night-flowering catchfly, *S.
noctiflora*, with long, narrow bracts below the 3/4-inch
flowers, which open at night and close during the day;
and white campion, *S. latifolia*, with 1-inch flowers, 5
styles, and sticky-hairy leaves and stems.

Daucus carota   June–September   Plate **7B**
Queen Anne's Lace,
Wild Carrot   Parsley (Carrot) Family

To distinguish Queen Anne's lace from the several
other species with flat-topped clusters of white flowers, look for the single 1/8-inch-wide purple flower in
the middle of a flat-topped compound umbel up to 5
inches wide. The leaves are pinnately divided and finely

dissected, giving them a fernlike appearance. The stem is bristly and may be 4 feet tall. When in fruit, the umbel curls up and resembles a bird's nest. The bristly seeds are dispersed by catching on the fur of passing mammals.

The central purple flower is said to represent a drop of the blood of Queen Anne, who pricked her finger while making lace.

This plant is the ancestor of the garden carrot and is also edible. The first-year roots are white and smaller and tougher than carrots, but have a similar flavor. The root is sometimes roasted and used as a coffee substitute. A root tea was traditionally used as a diuretic and to prevent and eliminate urinary stones. The seeds are a folk "morning after" contraceptive. Handling the plant causes photodermatitis in some people. As with other the species in this family, great care should be used in identifying the plant before it is handled or eaten.

Erigeron annuus   June–September   Plate **7C**
Daisy Fleabane   Aster Family

Daisy fleabane has 50 to 100 3/4-inch white, pinkish, or bluish flower heads with yellow disks in few to many terminal clusters. Fleabanes are similar to asters, but have more ray flowers. The alternate leaves are lanceolate to oval with sharp teeth. The upright stem is covered with perpendicular hairs. The plant grows to 5 feet tall. Daisy fleabane is an introduced annual whose seeds are produced without pollination.

A closely related species, lesser daisy fleabane, *E. strigosus*, is shorter, with fewer leaves with sparse or no teeth, and the stem hairs lie along the stem.

Daisy fleabane is common in open sunny areas throughout the Berkshires.

Anthemis cotula   July   Plate **7D**
Mayweed, Dog Fennel,
Stinking Chamomile   Aster Family
    Mayweed is a malodorous roadside weed with attractive 1-inch daisylike flowers. The flower heads have 10 to 16 white ray flowers and a domed yellow disk. The alternate leaves are finely divided and may be up 2 1/2 inches long. The plant is bushy and may be up to 2 feet tall.
    A tea was once brewed from mayweed for use as a diuretic and to induce sweating. The foliage was rubbed on the skin to relieve bee stings. The pioneers called the plant fever weed, and tradition has it that Johnny Appleseed planted it in the Ozarks after his wife and child died from the "chills." Several kinds of birds eat the seeds.
    Mayweed is found throughout the Berkshires in dry areas in fields and along roadsides.

Monotropa uniflora   July   Plate **7E**
Indian Pipe, Corpse Plant, Ice Plant   Pyrola Family
    Indian pipe might easily be mistaken for a tall, slender mushroom as it has no chlorophyll and its leaves are reduced to scales. Look for erect white to pink waxy stalks 3 to 10 inches tall with a solitary nodding flower. The flower is tubular, about 1 inch long, and has 5 petals. As the seed capsules mature, they become erect as the entire plant turns black. When fresh, the plant stands out against the dark forest floor. Indian pipe is parasitic on fungi which have a mycorrhizal relationship with other plants.
    Edible but tasteless, Indian pipe was used in the 19th century to treat inflamed eyes. The juice of the plant was

squeezed directly into the eyes or applied with a cloth dipped into water in which the plant had been soaked.

The species is widespread in shady moist woods. Look for it on Mount Greylock, on October Mountain, at Pleasant Valley Sanctuary, in Kennedy Park, at Bartholomew's Cobble, and at Notchview Reservation.

Pyrola elliptica   July   Plate **7F**
Shinleaf   Heath Family

Shinleaf is one of the more common of several similar, closely related plants found in wooded areas in the Berkshires. The 2/3-inch white, waxy flowers occur in loose clusters at the top of a leafless stem. They are nodding and fragrant, and have 5 petals and a contorted style which bends downward and curves upward at the tip. The evergreen leaves are dark olive green with reddish stalks, basal, elliptical, and rounded at the tip. They may be up to 2 3/4 inches long with the leaf blade longer than its stalk. The plant may reach 1 foot tall and spreads with creeping rhizomes.

Some American Indians used shinleaf to make shinplasters to dress wounds. It is astringent and has been used as a gargle, eyewash, and vaginal douche.

Shinleaf is found in dry and moist woods. Watch for it at Notchview Reservation, Pleasant Valley Sanctuary, Kennedy Park, and Bartholomew's Cobble.

Angelica atropurpurea   July–August   Plate **8A**
Purple-stem Angelica,
Alexanders   Parsley (Carrot) Family

A large, erect plant with small white to greenish flowers in spherical umbels up to 8 inches in diameter is probably purple-stem angelica. The leaves are alternate, long-stalked, and 2 or 3 times pinnately divided. The leaflets are toothed. The leaves have inflated bases which sheathe the stem. (*Heracleum lanatum*, cow parsnip, p. 14, has similar leaf bases, but its flowers occur in flat-topped umbels.) The stem is smooth, hollow, and purple or streaked with purple.

Parts of this plant are edible, but the plant can be confused with the poisonous water hemlock, *Cicuta maculata*, which also has purple markings on its stems and occurs in similar habitats. The generic name means angel; according to legend, the medicinal properties of related species were revealed to a monk by an angel during an outbreak of the plague. A tea made from purple angelica has been used to treat a variety of ailments. Some American Indians used the root to flavor smoking tobacco.

Purple-stem angelica is found in wet open areas throughout the Berkshires. You can find it on October Mountain, at Pleasant Valley Sanctuary, and at Bartholomew's Cobble.

Drosera rotundifolia   July–August   Plate **8B**
Round-leaved Sundew   Sundew Family

In boggy and peaty areas, watch for small, glistening, reddish rosettes of 1/2-inch circular leaves on 1 1/2-inch stems. If you kneel down and examine the leaves you will discover that they glisten because they are covered with glandular hairs, each of which has a droplet of sticky substance at its tip. The droplets contain digestive enzymes which break down the tissues of insects that become trapped on them. The insectivory of sundews is believed to be an adaptation to living on nutrient-poor soils.

In midsummer, 5-petaled flowers occur in 1-sided terminal clusters on leafless stems that may be as tall as 9 inches.

Sundews have been used in folk remedies for treating lung ailments and for removing corns and warts. The juice is sometimes used as a substitute for rennet to curdle milk.

Round-leaved sundew can be found on October Mountain and at Pleasant Valley Sanctuary.

Anaphalis margaritacea   July–September   Plate **8C**
Pearly Everlasting   Aster Family
Look for a stiff, erect woolly-white plant in open dry areas. Pearly everlasting flowers occur in flat clusters of 1/2 inch globular heads with white petallike bracts. There are no ray flowers, and the numerous disk flowers form a small central yellow tuft. Male and female flowers are found on separate plants. The entire plant is pubescent; the alternate, narrow leaves are gray green on top and quite cottony underneath. The leaves are up to 5 inches long and the plant may stand 3 feet tall.

American Indians and colonists used an astringent decoction of pearly everlasting to treat hemorrhoids. Currently, pearly everlasting is widely used as an ornamental for foliage contrast and for dried arrangements. There is considerable variation in the plants offered for sale and they often include foreign varieties of the native species as well as other species under one name.

Pearly everlasting is found throughout the Berkshires in dry open areas. Watch for it in the power line cut in Kennedy Park.

Eupatorium perfoliatum   July–September   Plate **8D**
Boneset, Thoroughwort   Aster Family
     The combination of dense, flat-topped clusters of
1/4-inch white flowers and opposite leaves joined at
the base are indicative of boneset. The leaves appear
wrinkled, are hairy underneath, and have long pointed
tips. The branched stem is hairy and may reach 5 feet
in height.
     Some American Indians used boneset to induce
sweat and treat fevers. Boneset was introduced from
North America into England in 1699 as a medicinal herb.
During the Civil War, Confederate troops drank a hot
infusion of the plant as a substitute for quinine. The
common name may come from its use to set broken
bones, a use indicated by the doctrine of signatures since
the leaves are joined at the base, or from the use of the
plant to treat dengue, also called break-bone fever.
     Boneset is found in damp areas throughout the
Berkshires. Watch for it around the base of Mount
Greylock, at Canoe Meadows, and at Pleasant Valley
Sanctuary.

Phytolacca americana   July–September   Plate **8E**
Pokeweed, Pokeberry   Pokeweed Family
     Pokeweed is a succulent plant that often looks like
a medium-sized shrub. The flowers are about 1/4 inch
wide, greenish white tinged with pink, and occur on
racemes up to 8 inches long which arise opposite the
leaves. The flowers have no petals and 5 petallike sepals. The fruits are 1/4-inch purple black berries with
red stems, which hang in drooping clusters. The alternate leaves are dark green, entire, elliptic to lanceolate,
tapering at both ends, long-stalked, and may be up to 1

foot long. The branching stem is thick and smooth, succulent, hollow, and purple-tinged. The plant may grow to 10 feet tall. When broken, the plant has a disagreeable odor.

This is a dangerous plant which has been cultivated as a garden vegetable in the United Sates and Europe. Before the red color appears in the plant in spring, the young shoots are cooked or pickled and the young leaves are cooked as greens. The fruit juice has been used as a food coloring and to tint cheap wine. It was also used as ink during the Civil War. Dyers use the berries to produce a red dye. Some American Indians made a tea of the berries to treat rheumatism and arthritis. The root, mature plant, and seeds have long been known to be poisonous and the juice can cause dermatitis. Recent studies have found that the plant contains mitogens which can be absorbed through skin abrasions and cause blood aberrations and damage chromosomes. Some medical authorities advise wearing gloves when handling the plant. In addition, the plant has been found to be an alternate host to cucumber mosaic disease. Bluebirds, mockingbirds, and cedar waxwings eat the berries with no apparent ill effects.

Pokeweed is common in the Berkshire along the edges of fields, woods, and roadsides.

Gaultheria procumbens   August   Plate **8F**
Wintergreen, Teaberry, Checkerberry   Heath Family
If you find a stand of low, shrubby plants with glossy, leathery, dark green oval leaves, crush one of the leaves in your fingers. If it has the pleasant spicy fragrance of wintergreen, it is probably this species. The flowers are white 5-lobed bells about 1/3 inch long.

They occur in nodding groups of 2 or 3 in the leaf axils. The leaves are evergreen and arranged alternately and usually clustered at the tips of the erect stems, which may grow to 6 inches tall. The fruit is a bright red berry about 1/4 inch wide.

The fruits are tasty and can be used as a trail snack. If plentiful they can be gathered to be used in muffins or made into jam. Dried leaves may be made into a tea. Wintergreen is one source of oil of wintergreen, the active ingredient of which is methyl salicylate. Most commercial oil of wintergreen is now made synthetically, however. In colonial times, children chewed the roots of wintergreen to prevent caries. Oil of wintergreen has long been used to treat rheumatism, headache, and fever. Prolonged use or large doses can cause stomach irritation. A search to find a similar drug without the side effects led Bayer to discover acetylsalicylic acid, which he named aspirin. Pure oil of wintergreen is poisonous except in very small amounts. The foliage is eaten by deer and ruffed grouse.

Wintergreen occurs commonly throughout the Berkshires on dry or moist acid wooded sites.

Aster

From August into November, asters are among the most common wildflowers in the Berkshires. Identifying them is tricky as some of the 20 species occurring here are very similar and can be separated only by using technical keys. However, many of the species can be tentatively identified by examining the shape and size of the leaves, whether the leaves clasp the stem, the color and size of the flowers, and habitat. Find the photograph which most closely matches the plant you are trying to identify and then read the species account for further guidance in identification.

Aster lateriflorus   August–September   Plate **9A**
Calico Aster, Side-flowering Aster   Aster Family
    Nine species of asters that occur in the Berkshires usually have white flowers. Often they can be identified by general characteristics, but because of the similarity among some species and variation within species, a technical key is necessary for positive identification. Calico aster is usually easy to identify by its shrubby habit and horizontal branches dotted with small flower heads held on one side of the stem. The flower heads are about 1/2 inch wide with white rays and disks that are yellow when fresh and turn pinkish or purple as they age. A single plant is usually covered with flowers with different-colored centers in a patchwork pattern, hence the name calico. The alternate leaves are lanceolate, coarsely toothed, and up to 6 inches long. The much-branched stem may reach 5 feet in height.
    Calico aster is found in fields, thickets, and along roads and trails throughout the area.
    Two species of aster with white flowers have leaves with a heart-shaped base and distinct petiole. Schreber's aster, *A. schreberi*, has basal leaves more than 3 inches wide and blooms in July and August, and is found on river banks; white wood aster, *A. divaricatus*, has basal leaves less than 3 inches wide, blooms in August and September, and is found in woods. White-topped aster, *A. paternus*, has stalked leaves without the heart-shaped base, only about 5 ray flowers, and is found in dry woods. Three other species have narrow leaves like calico aster: tall white aster, *A. simplex*, has flowers in a

panicle, whereas white wreath aster, *A. ericoides*, and heath aster, *A. pilosus*, have untoothed narrow leaves, are somewhat shrubby, and are found in dry areas; the two are separated by differences in the involucral bracts visible only with a hand lens or microscope. In whorled aster, *A. acuminatus*, the internodes (intervals of stem between the leaves) are so reduced that the leaves appear to grow in a tight whorl; this species is found in woods. The flower heads of flat-topped aster, *A. umbellatus*, are arranged in a corymb; this aster frequents wet to damp areas.

Cuscuta gronovii   August–September   Plate **9B**
Dodder, Strangleweed   Morning Glory Family

Dodder is easily recognized as a mass of yellow to orange strings covering other vegetation. It produces dense clusters of tiny, 5-lobed, bell-shaped white flowers. Its most obvious characteristic, however, are the threadlike, apparently leafless stems (actually the leaves are present as minute scales) which twine around other plants. Dodder has no chlorophyll and is an annual parasite on other plants. The seedlings grow roots, but these die when the stems contact and start to climb a host plant. At this point, rootlike structures called haustoria are produced which invade the host's vascular system. Dodder is often injurious to crop plants.

Cherokee Indians used dodder as a poultice for bruises. If taken internally, it is a harsh laxative and causes digestive disorders in livestock.

It is found in moist soil throughout the Berkshires. Three other species have been reported in the Berkshires, but the species are difficult to distinguish without a microscope.

Echinocystis lobata   August–September   Plate **9C**
Wild Cucumber, Balsam Apple   Gourd family
In August and September, roadside vegetation is often covered with dense patches of lacy white flowers. Closer inspection will reveal tall cones of 1/2-inch, 6-lobed greenish white flowers. The clusters occur on axillary stalks about 6 inches long and consist only of staminate (male) flowers. The pistillate (female) flowers occur on short axillary stalks and consist of 1 or a few flowers. Fruits start developing while the plant is still blooming. They are bladderlike, ovoid, to about 2 inches long, and are covered with bristles. The mature seeds are dark brown and resemble large watermelon seeds. The plant is an annual. The 5-lobed, toothed alternate leaves resemble maple leaves and are up to 3 1/2 inches long. The viny stem is grooved, with many branched tendrils; it grows over other vegetation and may reach 25 feet in length.

Wild cucumber is found on fence rows, roadsides, and stream banks throughout the Berkshires.

Some American Indians used a bitter root tea for a variety of ailments and as a love potion. The related tropical plant *Momordica balsamina*, also known as balsam apple, is highly toxic. Wild cucumber is sometimes planted to hide unsightly areas.

The similar 1-seeded bur cucumber, *Sicyos angulatus*, is found in similar habitats in the Berkshires. It has 5-petaled flowers and sticky, hairy stems. The 1/2-inch fruits are prickly, occur in small clusters, and each contains only 1 seed.

Polygonum cuspidatum   August–September   Plate **9D**
Japanese Knotweed,
Japanese Bamboo   Smartweed Family

A big clump of a stiff upright plant with large clusters of greenish white flowers may be Japanese knotweed. It is an aggressive, invasive plants and is usually found in dense stands. The flowers are about 1/8 inch wide, and occur in branching axillary clusters which may be up to 6 inches long. The flowers are either male or female and have sepals but no petals. The alternate leaves are oval with pointed tips and cordate bases and may be up to 6 inches long. The leaf base is enclosed in a membranous sheath that surrounds the stem. The zigzag, branching stem is thick and woody at the base, hollow, smooth, and often mottled. The plant may be up to 10 feet tall. The fruit is a triangular black, shiny nutlet.

The young shoots and rhizomes are edible, and the older stems can be used like rhubarb.

This plant is a garden escape that is difficult to eradicate. It is often found in neglected yards and gardens, in waste areas, and along moist roadsides. It can be found in Pleasant Valley Sanctuary, in Kennedy Park, and at Bartholomew's Cobble. There is a large stand of it across from the fire station in Interlaken.

Solidago bicolor   August–September   Plate **9E**
Silverrod   Aster Family

Silverrod is the easiest goldenrod to identify because its flowers are yellowish white. As soon as you realize you have a goldenrod, identification is automatic. Slender stalks up to 2 1/2 feet high bear alternate leaves, the lower ones of which are obviously toothed. The flowers occur on a long, cylindrical terminal spike.

Silverrod is found in rocky and sandy areas in open woods. A good stand of it grows near the lookout in Kennedy Park.

Eupatorium rugosum   August–October   Plate **9F**
White Snakeroot   Aster Family

Look for dense white fuzzy flower clusters on plants up to 4 feet tall with opposite, toothed, ovate leaves. The flower heads of white snakeroot consist solely of disk flowers, and the fuzz is the tips of the stamens.

This plant contains the toxic alcohol tremetol, responsible for milk sickness, which caused considerable loss of human life from colonial times into the 19th century. People became ill after drinking the milk of cows that had eaten white snakeroot; 10% to 25% of them died, including Nancy Hanks Lincoln, the mother of Abraham Lincoln.

This plant is abundant in shady areas in woods, in backyards, and fence rows, and along trails and roads. It blooms from late summer until frost.

Yellow to Orange Flowers

Tussilago farfara   March–April   Plate **11A**
Coltsfoot   Aster Family

Coltsfoot might be easily mistaken for an early dandelion as it is the first showy spring wildflower. The dandelionlike flower heads have numerous yellow ray flowers and appear before the leaves develop. They occur singly on reddish, scaly, unbranched stems. The leaves are basal, roundish, and shallowly lobed, and are said to resemble a colt's foot in outline. They have long stalks, are hairy underneath, and may be up to 8 inches long. The plant may grow as tall as 1 1/2 feet tall.

The young leaves and stalks may be eaten cooked as a potherb, and dried leaves can be used to make a fragrant tea. Candy or cough drops can be made by boiling the fresh leaves with sugar. Coltsfoot has been used to treat cough and respiratory problems, and in Europe, the dried leaves are smoked for cough and asthma.

Coltsfoot was introduced from Europe and is abundant in spring along Berkshire roadsides and stream banks and in wet meadows.

Viola   April–May
See Canada violet, *Viola canadensis*, p. 11, for help in identifying yellow violets.

Caltha palustris   April–June   Plate **11B**
Marsh Marigold, Cowslip   Buttercup Family

Marsh marigolds have bright, 1- to 1 1/2-inch-wide shiny yellow flowers, with 5 to 9 petallike sepals. The entire plant is succulent. The glossy leaves are long-stemmed, heart to kidney shaped, to 7 inches wide, and arranged alternately. Plants grow to about 2 feet tall and are found in wet areas in woods and meadows and in marshes and swamps. The seeds are spongy at one end, and this characteristic is thought to be an adaptation for dispersal by water.

The flowers were once used to color butter. The plant is poisonous when raw, but may be eaten cooked as a potherb. The flower buds are sometimes pickled and used as a substitute for capers. The juice has been used to treat warts. In Irish folklore, bunches of the plant were hung over doors on May Day to protect the fertility of cattle from witches and fairies.

Marsh marigolds can be found in wet areas throughout the Berkshires. The species is widely cultivated and double forms are available.

Erythronium americanum   April–June   Plate **11C**
Trout Lily, Dogtooth Violet,
Adder's Tongue   Lily Family

Watch for small lilies in spring and early summer. The nodding yellow flowers, which have 6 tepals curved backward, are about 1 1/2 inches long and occur singly on a leafless stalk. The outside of the tepals is usually brownish. The flowers may have yellow or maroon anthers, and some botanists think the two color phases represent two species. Plants are usually 8 to 10 inches tall with 2 tapering basal leaves that are mottled with brown or purple. It takes seven years for a seed to develop into a flowering plant; colonies of trout lily often contain many 1-leaved, nonflowering young plants. The seeds have a fleshy appendage that attracts ants, which then disperse the seeds.

The young leaves and bulbs are said to be edible; however, there are reports of the bulbs poisoning poultry. Iroquois women ate raw leaves as a contraceptive. Water extracts of the plant have been shown to be antibacterial.

Trout lilies can be found in moist wooded areas throughout the Berkshires.

Zizia aurea   April–June   Plate **11D**
Golden Alexanders   Parsley (Carrot) Family
The tiny 5-petaled yellow flowers of golden alexanders occur in a terminal umbel in which the central flower of each cluster is sessile. The leaves are arranged alternately and are 3-parted with finely toothed leaflets. The plant grows up to 2 1/2 feet tall. (See also the similar wild parsnip, *Pastinaca sativa*, p. 50.)

American Indians made a tea from the roots to treat fevers; however, the plant is considered to be toxic.

Golden alexanders is very common and widely distributed in the Berkshires in fields and open woods, on river banks, and along trails and roads.

Taraxacum officinale   April–September   Plate **11E**
Brown-seeded Dandelion, Blowballs   Aster Family
The cult of the perfect lawn has convinced many that dandelions are obnoxious plants. On the other hand, they are as handsome as many plants treasured in the

perennial border. The bright yellow flower heads, up to 2 1/2 inches wide, are found singly on smooth, hollow, leafless stalks. The flowers open in the morning and close in the evening; they remain closed on cloudy days. The leaves form a basal rosette, may be erect or flat on the ground, and can reach 16 inches long. They are hairy underneath and have irregular, backward-pointing teeth, which is the basis of the French name, dent de lion. The plant may reach 1 1/2 feet tall and has milky juice. Dandelions produce seed without pollination; thus, acres of them may be clones of one original plant.

The leaves, rich in vitamins A and C, can be used in salads and as potherbs. The flower heads are used to make dandelion wine. The roots may be roasted and ground to use as a coffee substitute. Tea made from the dried leaves has been used as a laxative, and the fresh roots have been used to treat liver, gallbladder, kidney, and bladder ailments. The flowers can be used to make a yellow dye and the roots, a magenta one.

Dandelions were introduced from Europe; in the Midwest, they have been deliberately cultivated as a food source for bees. The seeds are eaten by many birds, especially American goldfinches, *Carduelis tristis*. They are abundant in the Berkshires in nearly any open habitat.

Red-seeded dandelions, *T. laevigatum*, are also occasionally found in the Berkshires. They have somewhat smaller and paler flowers and more deeply cut leaves than brown-seeded dandelions, and red seeds.

Polygonatum biflorum   May   Plate **11F**
Giant Solomon's Seal   Lily Family
Giant Solomon's seal might be first noticed as a clump of arching stems up to 3 feet long. Look under-

neath for the 2 to several flowers dangling from the leaf axils. (In false Solomon's seal, *Smilacina racemosa*, the flowers form a terminal cluster; see p. 10.) The greenish yellow 1/2-inch flowers are bell-shaped and 6-lobed. The alternate leaves occur in 2 horizontal rows, one on each side of the stem; they are smooth with parallel veins, lanceolate to ovate with pointed tips, sessile or short-stalked, and may reach 4 inches in length. The undersides of the veins are smooth. The stems are unbranched; usually all the stems in a clump arch in the same direction.

The young shoots can be eaten cooked like asparagus. The rhizomes were eaten by some American Indians like potatoes. Some Indians also brewed the roots for tea to treat a variety of ailments. Eating the berries causes vomiting and diarrhea.

The origin of the plant's name is lost in history. One story claims that the leaf scars on the rhizomes resemble the six-pointed figure called Solomon's seal. Another holds that the Greeks used the roots for sealing wounds and healing broken bones and in doing so showed the wisdom of Solomon.

Solomon's seal, *P. pubescens*, is the more common species found in the Berkshires. It tends to be smaller than giant Solomon's seal, has hairs under the leaf veins, and usually has only 1 or 2 flowers at each node.

Solomon's seal is a common plant in Berkshire woods. Watch for it at Pleasant Valley Sanctuary and Bartholomew's Cobble.

Ranunculus recurvatus   May   Plate **12A**
Hooked Crowfoot   Buttercup Family
The crowfoots are less showy relatives of the buttercups and are easily overlooked. The shape of the usu-

ally compound leaves is said to resemble that of a crow's foot. They have small (to 3/8-inch) yellow or, in a few species, white flowers. Often the sepals are longer than the petals. At least seven species occur in the Berkshires.

The leaves of hooked crowfoot are not compound but rather deeply cleft into 3 oval segments. The flowers are pale yellow, about 1/2 inch wide, and have 5 petals no longer than the sepals. The leaves are toothed and the stems hairy. The plant may reach 2 feet in height. The plant gets its name from the hooks on the seeds.

This is a common Berkshire plant in damp woods. Watch for it at Pleasant Valley Sanctuary and Bartholomew's Cobble.

Barbarea vulgaris   May–June   Plate **10**
Winter Cress, Yellow Rocket   Mustard Family

In the spring, many plants in the Berkshires have bright yellow flowers. Those with 4-petaled flowers about 1/3 inch wide held in dense, cylindrical terminal clusters are probably winter cress. (Also compare greater celandine, p. 45.) This plant has a basal rosette of pinnately lobed leaves and toothed, ovate, clasping leaves arranged alternately on the smooth stems. The plant is erect and usually 2 to 3 feet high. The basal leaves are evergreen.

At the beginning of the 20th century, this species was widely sold by seed houses as an edible herb. Summer greens are too bitter to eat, but after frost and through the winter the tops can be used in salads or cooked. They were once used to make a tea to suppress coughs, but recent research indicates that they may cause kidney malfunction. The seeds are eaten by several species of birds.

Winter cress is found throughout the Berkshires in moist soil along roads and in fields and gardens.

Clintonia borealis   May–June   Plate **12B**
Bluebead Lily, Corn Lily   Lily Family
Bluebead lily is recognizable by its bell-like, nodding, greenish yellow flowers on bare stems up to 16 inches tall. The 6-petaled flowers are about 3/4 inch long, and 2 to several of them are clustered in a terminal umbel. There are 2 to 5 shiny, elliptical, entire, pointed basal leaves up to 15 inches long. The fruit is a dark blue berry about 3/8 inch in diameter. They are often eaten by chipmunks.

The very young leaves taste like cucumber and can be eaten fresh or cooked. In Maine, where they are widely eaten, they are known as cow-tongue. In our area the plant is not common enough to withstand much picking. Because the young leaves resemble those of some poisonous species they are best passed up. The berries are inedible and said to be poisonous.

Look for bluebead lily in rich woods on October Mountain, Mount Greylock, and Bartholomew's Cobble. There is a large patch of bluebead lily at the top of Lenox Mountain along the Pleasant Valley Sanctuary trails to the fire tower.

Medeola virginiana   May–June   Plate **12C**
Indian Cucumber Root   Lily Family
To find Indian cucumber root look for a stiff, upright plant about 2 feet tall with 2 whorls of leaves. The larger whorl of 5 to 9 lanceolate leaves occurs about halfway up the stem, and the smaller one of 3 leaflets is

at the top. The greenish yellow flowers, which occur in a terminal umbel of 3 to 9 flowers, often droop below the upper whorl of leaves. The flowers are 6-parted, about 1/2 inch long, and have protruding reddish styles and stamens. The fruit is a dark purplish berry on an erect stalk.

The rhizome tastes like cucumber and was widely eaten by American Indians and colonists either fresh or pickled. The species is not abundant enough for heavy use as food.

Indian cucumber root is found in moist woods on Mount Greylock and October Mountain.

Potentilla simplex   May–June   Plate **12D**
Common Cinquefoil,
Oldfield Cinquefoil   Rose Family
     Cinquefoils resemble strawberry plants but have yellow flowers. Common cinquefoil is a weak-stemmed plant with 1/2-inch, 5-petaled yellow flowers. The flowers are solitary on long axillary stalks. The alternate leaves may be up to 2 1/2 inches long and are palmately compound with 5 toothed leaflets. The branched stem is arching and prostrate. It may reach 3 1/2 feet in length, and roots at the nodes.

Common cinquefoil can survive on acid, sterile soil and is an indicator of impoverished land. Watch for it in dry areas such as old fields, roadsides, open woods, and waste areas.

Senecio aureus   May–June   Plate **12E**
Golden Ragwort, Squaw Weed   Aster Family
     Golden ragwort has 3/4-inch daisylike flowers with

8 to 12 yellow to orange rays and a yellow central disk. The heads occur in flat-topped terminal clusters. The basal leaves are long-stalked, rounded, heart shaped at the base, and up to 6 inches long; the stem leaves are alternate, pinnately lobed, and up to 3 1/2 inches long. The unbranched stem may reach 40 inches tall.

This species is found in moist soils in meadows, woods, bogs, and swamps.

Golden ragwort has been used by American Indians, settlers, and herbalists to promote menstruation and to hasten labor. Ragworts contain toxic pyrrolizidine alkaloids and have caused human poisonings, illness and death in livestock, and cancer in laboratory animals. Chronic use may cause liver disease.

Three other species of *Senecio* are found in the Berkshires. Round-leaved ragwort, *S. obovatus*, has egg-shaped leaves with tapered bases and is found in rocky areas; balsam ragwort, *S. pauperculus*, has lanceolate leaves and is found on calcareous ledges; and common groundsel, *S. vulgaris*, has no ray flowers and is an introduced weed often found in greenhouses and nursery stock.

Chelidonium majus　　　　　May–August　Plate **12F**
Greater Celandine, Swallowwort　　　　Poppy Family
Greater celandine has bright yellow flowers up to 2/3 inch wide arranged in loose clusters. It is readily distinguished from winter cress, *Barbarea vulgaris* (see p. 42), which blooms at about the same time and in similar habitats, by its larger flowers with numerous stamens, distinctive foliage, and yellow orange sap. The leaves are deeply pinnately lobed, whitish on their undersides, up to 8 inches wide, and arranged alternately

on the hairy, branched stems. The plant may grow to 2 1/2 feet tall.

Greater celandine was introduced from Europe, where it is said to begin blooming when the swallows return and to finish when the swallows depart in the fall. It is also said that swallows bathe the eyes of their young with the sap to improve their vision.

A decoction of the plant was used in England as a mouthwash for toothache and mixed with lard to treat hemorrhoids. The juice has been used to treat warts, corns, and ringworm, but it is highly irritating and may cause paralysis. The entire plant is poisonous, and people in Europe have died from it. It can be used as a yellow dye for wool.

This species grows along roadsides and in waste areas throughout the Berkshires.

Hieracium pilosella   June   Plate **13A**
Mouse-ear Hawkweed   Aster Family
Watch for rosettes of hairy oblong leaves about 5 inches long, often in large dense mats. The dandelionlike flowers, with yellow heads about 1 inch across, occur singly on hairy leafless stalks. The bracts of the flower heads are covered with black hairs. The flower stalks grow to about 1 foot tall or less.

Tea made from the leaves has been used to treat liver ailments and diarrhea.

This European introduction can be found in pastures, fields, and lawns. It is sometimes grown as a rock garden plant.

Galium verum   June–July   Plate **13B**
Our-Lady's Bedstraw,
Yellow Bedstraw   Madder Family

Our-Lady's bedstraw has dense terminal and axillary clusters of tiny, bright yellow flowers. The flowers
are 4-lobed and frequently fragrant. The narrow, 1-inch-
long, lanceolate leaves occur in whorls of 8 to 12. They
have a rough surface and are hairy underneath. The
stems are smooth and ridged; they are often prostrate
at first and then erect to about 3 feet tall.

A decoction of the plant has been used to curdle milk
in cheese making. A red dye may be made from the roots
and a yellow one, once used to color cheese, from the
flowers. The plant is fragrant when dried and once was
commonly used to stuff mattresses and pillows. One
legend holds that this plant was in the hay on which
Mary slept in Bethlehem. Tradition has it that a newly
married couple who sleep on a mattress filled with yellow bedstraw will have many children.

Our-Lady's bedstraw was introduced from Europe
and is common along Berkshire roadways and in pastures and fields in midsummer.

Lilium canadense   June–July   Plate **13C**
Canada Lily   Lily Family

Canada lily has yellow to orange nodding bell-
shaped flowers, with 1 to several on long stalks. The
flowers are 2 to 3 inches wide and consist of 3 petals
and 3 petallike sepals that are spotted on the inside. The
tips of the flowers arch outward, but not backward.
Plants have lanceolate leaves arranged in whorls of 4
to 10 on stems that may reach 5 feet in height. The leaves
may be 6 inches long and have minute prickles along

their margins.

Some American Indians cooked the bulbs to thicken soups and used the plant to treat snakebite.

Canada lily is a majestic plant which fortunately is common in moist areas in woods and along roadsides throughout the Berkshires. It can be found at Canoe Meadows, Pleasant Valley Sanctuary, and Bartholomew's Cobble.

Lysimachia ciliata   June–July   Plate **13D**
Fringed Loosestrife   Primrose Family

The genus *Lysimachia* is represented in the Berkshires by four native species and one hybrid as well as two species that have escaped from cultivation. All but one have yellow flowers with 5 petals, but they can be distinguished by differences in flower and leaf arrangement and a few other details mentioned below.

Fringed loosestrife has the largest flowers, about 3/4 inch wide, often with red markings at the center; it is the only species growing wild in our area in which the petals are toothed. The flowers occur on long stalks in the leaf axils. The leaves, 2 to 4 inches long, are ovate to lanceolate with a sharp tip and cordate base. The leaf petioles are fringed with hairs, a characteristic from which this species gets its name. The leaves are oppositely arranged on the squarish stems, which are often branched. The erect plant may grow to 4 feet tall. Fringed loosestrife is found throughout the Berkshires in moist areas in woods and thickets, and along streams and other water bodies. A purple-leaved variety is widely cultivated as an ornamental.

Whorled loosestrife, *L. quadrifolia*, is a similar erect species that also has flowers which arise in the leaf axils, but the lanceolate leaves are arranged in whorls of 4. The stems are usually unbranched, and the plant may grow to 2 1/2 feet tall. Whorled loosestrife is found in moist and dry open woods. It is abundant in the power line cut in Kennedy Park. Another similar species is swamp candles, *L. terrestris*, found in wet areas such as marshes, bogs, swamps, and meadows. Its flowers are arranged in a terminal spike which may be 10 inches long. The leaves are lanceolate, pointed at both ends, and arranged oppositely. Purple bulbils develop in the upper leaf axils in late summer. Whorled loosestrife and swamp candles have red markings on their petals and occasionally hybridize to yield plants which combine their characteristics. Tufted loosestrife, *L. thyrsiflora*, looks quite different from the preceding species. Its flowers have 6 very narrow petals which are grouped in rounded tufted globes in the leaf axils. It is found in marshes.

The introduced species include garden loosestrife, *L. vulgaris*, which is downy and has flowers with no red markings in terminal spikes, and moneywort, *L. nummularia*, which is a creeping prostrate plant with flowers in the leaf axils.

Nuphar variegata   June–July   Plate **13E**
Spatterdock, Yellow Pond Lily   Water Lily Family
A large, floating buttercup would be a good description of the flower of spatterdock. The flowers are cuplike and up to 3 inches wide. They have 5 or 6 fleshy, petallike sepals, many stamenlike petals, numerous stamens, and a disklike stigma. The floating leaves are heart shaped with rounded tips, have overlapping basal lobes, and may be 1 foot long. The leaf stalks may be as

long as 12 feet.

The seeds may be cooked and eaten whole or ground into flour and used like cornmeal. The rhizomes may be boiled and used like potatoes or dried and ground into flour. The seeds are eaten by waterfowl and marsh birds; moose, beaver, and porcupines eat the plants.

Spatterdock may be found in the Berkshires on ponds, shallow lakes, and slow-moving streams.

Small pond lily, *N. microphylla*, a similar species with flowers up to 1 inch wide and leaves up to 4 inches long, is a rare plant in the Berkshires.

Pastinaca sativa   June–July   Plate **13F**
Wild Parsnip   Parsley (Carrot) Family

Wild parsnip grows to about 5 feet tall and has tiny, 5-petaled yellow flowers growing in a flat-topped umbel. (See golden alexanders, *Zizia aurea*, for comparison; p. 39.) A good clue to identification of this plant is the deeply grooved stem along with alternate pinnately compound leaves with 5 to 15 toothed or lobed leaflets.

Wild parsnip was introduced from Europe and is the parent of the cultivated parsnip. Its taproot is edible but slender and usually tough and stringy. It is best to avoid eating wild plants because of the possibility of confusing them with the poisonous water hemlock, *Cicuta maculata*, the root of which smells like parsnips. Both the wild and the cultivated forms of parsnip can cause contact dermatitis and photodermatitis due to the presence of xanthotoxin, sometimes used to treat psoriasis and vitiligo.

This plant is found throughout our area in sunny sites in fields and waste areas and along roads and trails.

Ranunculus bulbosus   June–July   Plate **14A**
Bulbous Buttercup   Buttercup Family
   Buttercups have bright golden yellow flowers with 5 glossy petals occurring solitarily or in terminal clusters.
   Bulbous buttercup is easily distinguished by sepals that fold down against the stem and a bulblike thickening at the base of the leaves. There are few alternate stem leaves. The basal leaves have long stalks and 3 dissected segments, the middle one of which is stalked. The stems are hairy, and the plant may grow to 2 feet tall.
   Bulbous buttercup was introduced from Europe and is common in fields, meadows, lawns, and along roadsides.
   The "bulb" is said to be edible as an emergency food if cooked in several changes of water. The fresh foliage is acrid and can cause blistering of the mouth and intestinal tract if eaten. Cows eating fresh plants produce unpalatable reddish milk.
   Four other species commonly called buttercups occur in the Berkshires. All have spreading sepals. Yellow water buttercup, *R. flabellaris*, is an aquatic plant of only occasional occurrence. The other three terrestrial species are all common. Hispid buttercup, *R. hispidus*, lacks the basal swelling, and each of its main leaf segments are stalked; creeping buttercup, *R. repens*, is a creeping plant usually found in damp areas; and tall buttercup, *R. acris*, is a tall plant with leaves divided into 3 to 7 deeply cleft, stalkless segments.

Rhinanthus crista-galli   June–July   Plate **14B**
Yellow Rattle   Figwort Family
   One of the most distinctive characteristics of yellow rattle is the flower's flattened, inflated calyx. The 1/2-

inch flowers are yellow with 2 lips. The upper lip is arched and the lower 3-lobed. The flowers are stalkless and occur on a 1-sided spike; the bracts below the flowers have bristly teeth. The rough opposite leaves are triangular-lanceolate to oblong, toothed, sessile, and up to 2 1/2 inches long. The plant may reach 2 1/2 feet tall. The fruit is enclosed in the inflated calyx, and the seeds rattle in their capsule.

Yellow rattle is a parasite on the roots of other plants, usually grasses. It is now common in disturbed sites such as roadsides, especially in the northern Berkshires. It is common in the grassy area on the top of Mount Greylock and around the entrance road to Notchview Reservation.

Trifolium aureum   June–July   Plate **14C**
Hop Clover   Pea Family

A short plant bearing little yellow pompons may be hop clover. The individual pealike flowers are about 1/4 inch long and occur in roundish to oblong heads 1/2 to 1 inch wide growing in the leaf axils. The alternate leaves are palmately compound with 3 wedge-shaped leaflets 1/2 to 1/3 inch long. The erect stems are branched and smooth, and may reach 16 inches in height.

Hop clover was introduced from Europe and is used as a cover crop for poor soils. You'll find it throughout the Berkshires in fields and along roadsides.

The similar low hop clover, *T. campestre*, has somewhat smaller heads and leaves and a prostrate stem. Black medick, *Medicago lupulina*, another yellow-flowered member of the pea family, is a sprawling plant with flower heads that are smaller and brighter colored than the hop clovers. Its leaflets are tipped with a short bristle. Rabbit-foot clover, *T. arvense*, is similar to hop clover but has pinkish gray flowers and narrow, hairy leaflets.

Hemerocallis fulva   June–August   Plate **14D**
Daylily   Lily Family

Daylilies were introduced from Europe and are found nearly everywhere throughout the Northeast where there has been human activity. Watch for them along the roadsides, around old home sites, and in any area where someone might have dumped yard refuse.

The 4-inch-wide orange flowers are funnel-shaped, face upward or outward, and have 6 brightly colored backward-curving segments: 3 petals and 3 sepals, each with a pale stripe down the center. The flowers occur in terminal clusters on leafless stems and each lasts only a day. The 3-foot-long leaves, growing from the base of the plant, are grasslike and have a distinct central crease. This species is believed to be a hybrid; it is sterile and produces no seed. Clumps spread slowly by rhizomes, but colonize new areas only when moved by human activity.

The young shoots can be used in salads or cooked like asparagus. The flower buds are a staple of Oriental cuisine and used fresh or dried in soups, stir fries, etc. Fresh flowers can be dipped in fritter batter and deep-fried. The tubers when cooked are reported to taste like corn; however, recent studies in China indicate that frequent consumption of them leads to accumulation of a toxin which can cause blindness.

Linaria vulgaris   June–August   Plate **14E**
Butter-and-Eggs, Toadflax   Figwort Family

This species looks like miniature bright yellow snapdragons. The flowers are 2-lipped, the upper lip being 2-lobed and the lower 3-lobed with a orange palatelike projection. They are about 1 inch long, have a long spur, and occur in dense terminal spikes. The gray green leaves are very narrow, almost grasslike, 1 to 2 1/2 inches long, and arranged alternately on the stiff, smooth stems. The plants may grow to 3 feet tall.

Butter-and-eggs was introduced from Europe and is sometimes called toadflax because it is a pest in flax fields there. It has been used as a diuretic and purgative. An ointment made from the flowers has been used to treat hemorrhoids and skin eruptions. The juice mixed with milk has been used as a fly poison, and an infusion of the leaves is sometimes fed to chickens as a spring tonic.

Butter-and-eggs is common along roadsides, in fields, and in waste areas throughout our area.

Oenothera biennis   June–August   Plate **14F**
Common Evening Primrose   Evening Primrose Family

The species of *Oenothera* come in two types; those in which the flowers are open during the day are called sundrops, and those in which the flowers are open overnight are called evening primroses. The Berkshire flora boasts one species of each kind.

Common evening primrose has numerous 2-inch yellow flowers at the ends of the stems and branches. There are 4 petals and 4 turned-back sepals, and the stigma is cross shaped. The flowers, which are lemon scented, open in the evening and fade by the following afternoon. This is a tall (to 6 feet), erect, hairy plant that is often tinged with red. The leaves, 3 to 7 inches long, are lanceolate with pointed tips and shallow teeth.

Common evening primrose is a biennial. The first-year roots are some times cooked as a vegetable. The young leaves are also edible but quite bitter. Common evening primrose has been used to treat respiratory ailments, and research has found that the oil may be useful in treating atopic dermatitis.

Common evening primrose is common along roadsides and in fields and waste areas. It can be found throughout the Berkshires; look for it at Pleasant Valley Sanctuary and Bartholomew's Cobble.

Small sundrops, *O. perennis*, is a shorter (to about 2 feet), less coarse plant than common evening primrose. The flowers are about 3/4 inch wide, and the leaves are entire and blunt ended.

Potentilla recta   June–August   Plate **15A**
Sulphur Cinquefoil,
Rough-fruited Cinquefoil   Rose Family

Sulphur cinquefoil has pale yellow 1-inch flowers with 5 notched petals. The flowers occur in flat-topped terminal clusters. The alternate leaves are palmately compound, the lower leaves 5 to 7 1-inch leaflets and the upper ones, 3 smaller leaflets. The leaflets are narrow, toothed, and hairy underneath. The stem is stout and hairy, and the plant may reach 2 feet in height.

Sulphur cinquefoil was introduced from Europe. It is now a troublesome pasture weed because livestock won't eat it and it spreads. It is found throughout the Berkshires in dry areas such as fields, pastures, roadsides, and waste areas.

Tragopogon pratensis   June–August   Plate **15B**
Yellow Goat's Beard, Meadow Salsify   Aster Family

A tall plant with a flower head resembling a dandelion may be yellow goat's beard. The solitary, terminal yellow flower heads are up to 2 1/2 inches wide, consist only of ray flowers, and are subtended by 8 green pointed bracts. The flowers open in the morning on sunny days and close by noon. The seed head looks like that of a giant dandelion. The alternate leaves are grasslike and clasp the stems; they may be up to 1 foot long. The stem is smooth and often branched. The plant may reach 3 feet tall and contains milky juice.

The young stems may be eaten raw or cooked. The first-year roots when cooked are said to taste like oysters or parsnips. The roots are sometimes roasted and ground and used as a coffee substitute. Yellow goat's beard is related to salsify or oyster plant, *T. porrifolius*, which is often grown as a vegetable. It was used in Europe and by some American Indians to treat heartburn.

Watch for this European introduction on roadsides and in fields and meadows in the Berkshires.

Hieracium aurantiacum   June–September   Plate **15C**
Devil's Paintbrush, Orange Hawkweed   Aster Family

Bright orange to red 3/4-inch flower heads distinguish this species. The flower heads occur in few to several terminal clusters held on leafless stems and consist solely of ray flowers. There is a basal rosette of elliptical leaves. The entire plant is hairy and may grow to 2 feet in height.

Devil's paintbrush is an alpine plant introduced from Eurasia. It thrives in open dry areas with poor soil. You'll see it frequently on roadsides and in lawns.

Matricaria matricarioides   June–September   Plate **15D**
Pineapple Weed   Aster Family
    Pineapple weed gets its name from the odor it gives off when bruised. The flowers are 1/4-inch cones, consisting only of disk flowers, at the ends of the branches. The leaves are finely divided and may be up to 2 inches long; the stems, smooth and often branched, may be either upright or sprawling. The plant may grow up to 16 inches tall, but is usually only a few inches high. Pineapple weed is a native of the Pacific Coast which has been introduced to the East.
    Blackfoot Indians used the dried flower heads as an insect repellent. Fresh or dried flower heads can be used to make a tea, similar to chamomile tea. Those who suffer from hay fever, however, may be allergic to it.
    Pineapple weed is found on roadsides and waste areas throughout our area.

Oxalis stricta   June–September   Plate **15E**
Yellow Wood Sorrel, Sour Grass   Wood Sorrel Family
    A small plant with clover-shaped leaves and bright 1/2-inch 5-petaled flowers is probably yellow wood sorrel. The flowers are on slender stalks in terminal or axillary clusters of 2 to 6. The leaves are palmately divided into 3 heart-shaped 1/2- to 3/4-inch-long leaflets. The leaflets, which are often purplish underneath, close at dusk and open at dawn. They are alternate on the branched, hairy stems. Plants may grow to 15 inches tall but are frequently much smaller.
    The leaves are sour tasting and are tempting to nibble on; however, they shouldn't be eaten in large quantities because they contain oxalates, which are poisonous.
    This is a common dooryard weed and is easy to find

in gardens, lawns, and along roadsides.

Rudbeckia hirta   June–September   Plate **15F**
Black-eyed Susan   Aster Family
It hardly seems necessary to describe this familiar plant. The flower heads, which may be up to 3 inches wide, consist of 8 to 20 golden yellow rays and a domed purplish brown disk. The heads are terminal and solitary. The alternate leaves are lanceolate to ovate, slightly toothed, hairy, and 2 to 7 inches long. The lower leaves have 3 prominent veins and winged petioles. The stem is usually unbranched and bristly. The plant may grow to 3 1/2 feet tall. Some American Indians made a tea from the plant to treat worms and colds, and they used the juice of the root to treat earaches. Black-eyed Susan can cause contact dermatitis. Livestock that eat it may experience loss of coordination, abdominal pain, and aimless wandering.

Black-eyed Susan puts on a good show along roadways and in meadows and fields throughout the Berkshires. It is widely cultivated, and many varieties are available.

Verbascum thapsus   June–September   Plate **16A**
Common Mullein, Flannel Plant,
Aaron's Rod   Figwort Family
To find common mullein, look for tall yellow candles growing out of woolly basal rosettes of large leaves. The dense club-shaped terminal clusters bear individual flowers that are 3/4 to 1 inch wide and have 5 irregular lobes. These open only a few at a time and last for only one day. The alternate stem leaves are thick and densely

covered with gray green wool and arise from a large basal rosette. The largest of the basal leaves may be 1 foot long. The plant is erect, usually unbranched, and may be up to 6 1/2 feet tall.

Common mullein, introduced from Europe, is a biennial. During its first year, it produces a basal rosette of leaves, and in the second year produces a flowering stalk. It is usually found in dry, gravelly, disturbed soils along roadsides and in neglected areas. The seeds pass undamaged through the intestinal tract of cattle.

The dried leaves have been brewed into a tea to treat coughs, hoarseness, and bronchitis. An ointment made by boiling the leaves in lard has been used to treat skin irritations and hemorrhoids. The dried foliage was smoked by American Indians and settlers to treat asthma. The leaves have been used to insulate shoes and moccasins. Romans soaked the flower stalks in tallow to use as torches and the Greeks used them as lamp wicks. The seeds contain rotenone and have been used as a fish poison.

Common mullein is a common plant along open roadsides throughout the Berkshires. Moth mullein, *V. blattaria*, another introduction from Europe, is occasionally found in the Berkshires. It has yellow or white flowers in an open, loose raceme and smooth, toothed leaves.

Hypericum perforatum   July–August   Plate **16B**
St. John's Wort, Klamathweed   St. John's Wort Family
    St. John's wort is a stiff, upright plant with terminal clusters of 1-inch-wide, 5-petaled yellow flowers. A distinctive feature of the family are the numerous stamens forming small tufts in the center of each flower. The leaves are oblong and if held up to the light can be seen

to have numerous translucent dots. They are opposite and sessile on the many-branched stems. There is a small ridge on the stem below each leaf.

This species was introduced from Europe. It has been used to treat a variety of ailments and was once used as a charm against witchcraft. If taken internally, it causes photosensitization of the skin leading to blisters. In western states, this plant has poisoned countless livestock. Hypericums are being studied for possible treatment of AIDS.

Lotus corniculatus   July–August   Plate **16C**
Bird's Foot Trefoil   Pea Family
Watch for shrubby mounds with bright yellow pea-like flowers in mid- to late summer. The flowers of bird's foot trefoil occur in umbels of 3 to 10 flowers at the tips of erect stems. The leaves are pinnately compound, consisting of 3 leaflets with 2 leafletlike stipules. The stem is branched and sprawling and may be 2 feet long. The clusters of the slender 1 1/2-inch-long seed pods are said to resemble bird's feet.

Bird's foot trefoil was introduced from Europe as a pasture plant that also makes good hay and silage. It is often used to stabilize slopes and road cuts and as an ornamental ground cover. It can be used to make blue and yellow dyes.

It is common throughout the Berkshires, often turning entire fields bright yellow.

Tanacetum vulgare   July–August   Plate **16D**
Tansy, Scented Fern   Aster Family
Tansy can be recognized by its flat-topped terminal

clusters of many 1/2-inch buttonlike yellow flower heads and its fernlike, aromatic foliage. The leaves are 1 or 2 times pinnately divided and many be up to 8 inches long. The stem is erect and smooth. The plant grows to about 3 1/2 feet tall.

Tansy was once used to flavor cheese and the leaves and flowers used as a substitute for sage. In England, the leaves are used to flavor tansy cakes, which are eaten at Lent. The bitter taste is said to symbolize Christ's suffering. It has been used to treat intestinal worms, to promote menstruation, and as an abortifacient. It has been implicated in abortion in cattle. In the Middle Ages, the tops were strewn on the floor to keep ants away. It was also hung in rafters, stored with bedclothes, and tucked in mattresses. In powdered form, it has been used as an insecticide. Research has shown the plant to be antispasmodic and antiseptic. Currently it is illegal in the United States to sell tansy as food or medicine.

Tansy is widespread in the Berkshires; it may be found along roads and in fields and gardens. It is often grown as an ornamental and used in dried flower arrangements.

Silphium perfoliatum   August   Plate **16E**
Cup Plant, Rosin Weed   Aster Family
Cup plant is a large, coarse plant with a flower head resembling a sunflower. The flower heads may be as much as 3 inches wide and consist of 20 to 30 yellow ray flowers with a yellow disk. They occur as few to several in terminal clusters. The ray flowers are fertile and the disk flowers sterile: just the opposite of sunflowers. The opposite leaves are coarsely toothed and may reach 8 inches wide by 1 foot long. The upper

leaves are fused at the bases, forming a cup around the stem. The much-branched stem is smooth and square. The plant may grow to 8 feet tall. Cup plant has resinous juice which oozes out and dries into a gummy mass.

The hardened juice is used as a natural chewing gum that is said to sweeten the breath. Some American Indians and early settlers used the gum to clean their teeth. Some American Indians burned the roots and inhaled the smoke to treat colds.

Cup plant has been introduced into the Berkshires from farther west. It can be found in moist woods and thickets and along steams and roads. It can be found at Canoe Meadows and at the picnic area in Kennedy Park.

Sonchus asper   August   Plate **16F**
Spiny-leaved Sowthistle   Aster Family

The flowers of spiny-leaved sowthistle resemble those of dandelions: the heads are yellow, consist solely of ray flowers, and are up to 1 inch wide. They occur in small terminal clusters. The alternate spiny-toothed leaves with few if any lobes clasp the stem and may be up to 10 inches long. The rounded, earlike projections at the base of the leaves are one of the best distinguishing characteristics. The stem is smooth, and the plant may reach 6 feet tall.

The young plants are bitter but edible after the spines have been removed.

The similar field sowthistle, *S. arvensis*, has flower heads more than 1 inch wide and clasping lobed leaves without earlike projections. The common sowthistle, *S. oleraceus*, has lobed leaves that usually have large, triangular terminal lobes. The three species are found in waste areas and along roadways throughout the Berkshires.

Abutilon theophrasti   August–September   Plate **17A**
Velvetleaf, China Jute   Mallow Family
    The 1-inch, 5-petaled yellow flowers of velvet leaf
last only about half a day. One or a few flowers are found
on axillary stalks. The fruit is cup shaped with a ring of
prickles around the rim of the cup. The alternate leaves
are heart shaped and pointed and covered with hairs.
They may be up to 10 inches long. The erect thick stem
may grow to 5 feet in height.
    Velvetleaf was introduced from Asia as a potential
fiber crop and is found in waste areas, gardens, and
fields. Although an annual, it is hard to eradicate since
the seed can remain viable for 50 years.
    The Chinese prepared a tea to treat dysentery from
the dried leaves and made a poultice of the plant to treat
ulcers. The stems are used in China to produce fibers
for rugs.
    Velvetleaf can best be found around the edges of
cornfields or in fields left fallow.

Bidens cernua   August–September   Plate **17B**
Nodding Bur Marigold, Stick-tight   Aster Family
    Nodding bur marigold is one of the showier of sev-
eral species of *Bidens* found in the Berkshires. Its flower
heads are up to 1 1/2 inches wide with 6 to 8 yellow
rays. The heads at first face outward but nod as they
age. This is an erect branched plant up to 3 1/2 feet tall,
with narrow, lanceolate, toothed leaves up to 6 inches
long oppositely arranged on the stems.
    Nodding bur marigold is an annual found in wet ar-
eas such as pond margins and roadside ditches. Its fruits
end in 4 barbed prongs that stick to clothing and fur.

Euthamia graminifolia August–September Plate **17C**
Lance-leaved Goldenrod,
Grass-leaved Goldenrod Aster Family
See the entry for *Solidago*, p. 65, for an overview of goldenrods. The species with flat-topped (corymbiform) clusters of flower heads have been placed in a separate genus, *Euthamia*. The individual heads are yellow and about 1/5 inch wide. The leaves are long, narrow (about 1/4 inch wide), and pointed. Plants may reach 4 feet tall and have smooth or downy stems that are branched above the middle.

Lance-leaved goldenrod is common in fields, on roadsides, and in power line cuts.

Helianthus decapetalus August–September Plate **17D**
Thin-leaved Sunflower Aster Family
Sunflowers growing in the woods are likely to be this species. Terminal branches bear several flower heads, each about 3 inches wide with a yellow disk. The plant is up to 5 feet tall with opposite, toothed lower leaves. The leaves are smooth and thin and have winged petioles.

The seeds are too small to provide much of a snack, but many species of wildlife eat them. American Indians roasted and ground the seeds into a meal used in breads and soups as well as using the unopened buds as a vegetable.

Look for this species in open areas in the woods.

Impatiens capensis August–September Plate **17E**
Spotted Jewelweed Touch-me-not Family
Spotted jewelweed has funnel-shaped orange, red-

dish-spotted, 3-petaled flowers with slender, curled basal spurs. The flowers dangle on thin axillary stalks. The leaves are pale green, long-stalked, ovate, and coarsely toothed. The upper leaves tend to be alternate while the lower ones are opposite. The stems are succulent and are usually branched. Plants may grow to 5 feet tall and often form dense stands. The ripe seed capsules burst explosively at the slightest touch, hurling the seeds in all directions.

The young plants can be used as a potherb, but because they contain calcium oxalate crystals, they should not be eaten frequently. The seeds are said to taste like walnuts or butternuts and make a good trail snack. The juice is widely used to prevent or treat poison ivy rash. Research has shown that it is an effective antifungal and it is used in some over-the-counter preparations. Ruby-throated hummingbirds, *Archilochus colubris*, feed on the nectar and are thought to be an important pollinator.

This plant can be found throughout the Berkshires wherever there is damp ground. The similar pale jewelweed, *I. pallida*, has yellow flowers and is often found in areas with neutral to basic soils.

Solidago

The goldenrods are a major component of the late summer and fall wildflower display. There are about 55 species in two genera in the northeastern United States; 22 species, of which about half are common, have been recorded in Berkshire County. Goldenrods belong to the aster family and the flower clusters are composed of groups of small daisylike flower heads. Except for one white species they are all yellow.

Goldenrods are sometimes erroneously cited as a

cause of hay fever, but the pollen is sticky and transported by bees rather than the wind; hay fever sufferers are thus not normally exposed to the pollen. The seeds are tufted and spread by the wind. The stems frequently have round swellings. These are galls caused by fly larvae which live and feed in them. In the winter, birds often peck open the galls for food. Goldenrods contain the compound quercitin, which is used in treating the kidney disease hemorrhagic nephritis. Goldenrod harvested along with hay has been blamed for poisoning sheep.

The nature of the underground parts, characters of the leaves and their distribution, and form of the inflorescences are used to separate the species. Identification of goldenrods to the species level is beyond the scope of this book. The species included here are chosen to give you an idea of the variation among goldenrods and tempt you to learn more about them. Goldenrods can be used to produce yellow or greenish yellow dyes for wool.

Solidago canadensis   August–October   Plate **17F**
Canada Goldenrod, Tall Goldenrod   Aster Family
Canada goldenrod is one of our most common species. The flowers are held in a dense, triangular terminal panicle. From a distance, it looks like a stubby cone at the top of the plant. Close examination will show that the flowers are attached to only one side of the branches and the lower ones arch sideways.

American Indians used this species as a tea to treat fevers and chewed the seeds for sore throats. Several cultivars of this plant are used as ornamentals.

Look for this species in open areas such as pastures, fields, fence rows, and waste places.

White to Cream

1 *Sanguinaria canadensis*
Bloodroot

2A *Alliaria petiolata*
Garlic Mustard

2B *Cardamine (Dentaria) diphylla*
Two-leaved Toothwort

2C *Dicentra cucullaria*
Dutchman's Breeches

2D *Saxifraga virginiensis*
Early Saxifrage

2E *Fragaria vesca*
Wood Strawberry

2F *Mitella diphylla*
Miterwort

3A *Actaea alba*
White Baneberry

3B *Anemone quinquefolia*
Wood Anemone

3C *Anthriscus sylvestris*
Wild Chervil

3D *Aralia nudicaulis*
Wild Sarsaparilla

3E *Trillium undulatum*
Painted Trillium

3F *Antennaria neglecta*
Pussytoes

4A *Cornus canadensis*
Bunchberry

4B *Smilacina racemosa*
False Solomon's Seal

4C *Tiarella cordifolia*
Foamflower

4D *Trientalis borealis*
Starflower

4E *Viola canadensis*
Canada Violet

4F *Calla palustris*
Wild Calla

5A *Heracleum lanatum*
Cow Parsnip

5B *Maianthemum canadense*
Canada Mayflower

5C *Apocynum cannabinum*
Indian Hemp

5D *Geum canadense*
White Avens

5E *Leucanthemum vulgare*
Oxeye Daisy

5F *Melilotus alba*
White Sweet Clover

6A *Stellaria aquatica*
Giant Chickweed

6B *Thalictrum pubescens*
Tall Meadow Rue

6C *Valeriana officinalis*
Common Valerian

6D *Achillea millefolium*
Yarrow

6E *Chelone glabra*
Turtlehead

6F *Nymphaea odorata*
Fragrant Water Lily

7A *Silene vulgaris*
Bladder Campion

7B *Daucus carota*
Queen Anne's Lace

7C *Erigeron annuus*
Daisy Fleabane

7D *Anthemis cotula*
Mayweed

7E *Monotropa uniflora*
Indian Pipe

7F *Pyrola elliptica*
Shinleaf

8A *Angelica atropurpurea*
Purple-stem Angelica

8B *Drosera rotundifolia*
Round-leaved Sundew

8C *Anaphalis margaritacea*
Pearly Everlasting

8D *Eupatorium perfoliatum*
Boneset

8E *Phytolacca americana*
Pokeweed

8F *Gaultheria procumbens*
Wintergreen

9A *Aster lateriflorus*
Calico Aster

9B *Cuscuta gronovii*
Dodder

9C *Echinocystis lobata*
Wild Cucumber

9D *Polygonum cuspidatum*
Japanese Knotweed

9E *Solidago bicolor*
Silverrod

9F *Eupatorium rugosum*
White Snakeroot

Yellow to Orange

10 *Barbarea vulgaris*
Winter Cress

11A *Tussilago farfara*
Coltsfoot

11B *Caltha palustris*
Marsh Marigold

11C *Erythronium americanum*
Trout Lily

11D *Zizia aurea*
Golden Alexanders

11E *Taraxacum officinale*
Brown-seeded Dandelion

11F *Polygonatum biflorum*
Giant Solomon's Seal

12A *Ranunculus recurvatus*
Hooked Crowfoot

12B *Clintonia borealis*
Bluebead Lily

12C *Medeola virginiana*
Indian Cucumber Root

12D *Potentilla simplex*
Common Cinquefoil

12E *Senecio aureus*
Golden Ragwort

12F *Chelidonium majus*
Greater Celandine

13A *Hieracium pilosella*
Mouse-ear Hawkweed

13B *Galium verum*
Our Lady's Bedstraw

13C *Lilium canadense*
Canada Lily

13D *Lysimachia ciliata*
Fringed Loosestrife

13E *Nuphar variegata*
Spatterdock

13F *Pastinaca sativa*
Wild Parsnip

14A *Ranunculus bulbosus*
Bulbous Buttercup

14B *Rhinanthus crista-galli*
Yellow Rattle

14C *Trifolium aureum*
Hop Clover

14D *Hemerocallis fulva*
Daylily

14E *Linaria vulgaris*
Butter-and-Eggs

14F *Oenothera biennis*
Common Evening Primrose

15A *Potentilla recta*
Sulfur Cinquefoil

15B *Tragopogon pratensis*
Yellow Goat's Beard

15C *Hieracium aurantiacum*
Devil's Paintbrush

15D *Matricaria matricarioides*
Pineapple Weed

15E *Oxalis stricta*
Yellow Wood Sorrel

15F *Rudbeckia hirta*
Black-eyed Susan

16A *Verbascum thapsus*
Common Mullein

16B *Hypericum perforatum*
St. John's Wort

16C *Lotus corniculatus*
Bird's Foot Trefoil

16D *Tanacetum vulgare*
Tansy

16E *Silphium perfoliatum*
Cup Plant

16F *Sonchus asper*
Spiny-leaved Sowthistle

17A *Abutilon theophrasti*
Velvetleaf

17B *Bidens cernua*
Nodding Bur Marigold

17C *Euthamia graminifolia*
Lance-leaved Goldenrod

17D *Helianthus decapetalus*
Thin-leaved Sunflower

17E *Impatiens capensis*
Spotted Jewelweed

17F *Solidago canadensis*
Canada Goldenrod

Pink to Red

18 *Polygala paucifolia*
Fringed Polygala

19A *Epigaea repens*
Trailing Arbutus

19B *Claytonia caroliniana*
Spring Beauty

19C *Trillium erectum*
Red Trillium

19D *Asarum canadense*
Wild Ginger

19E *Aquilegia canadensis*
Columbine

19F *Cardamine pratensis*
Cuckoo Flower

20A *Cypripedium acaule*
Pink Lady's Slipper

20B *Geranium maculatum*
Wild Geranium

20C *Pedicularis canadensis*
Wood Betony

20D *Streptopus roseus*
Rosy Twisted Stalk

20E *Hesperis matronalis*
Dame's Rocket

20F *Lychnis flos-cuculi*
Ragged Robin

21A *Sarracenia purpurea*
Pitcher Plant

21B *Oxalis acetosella*
Wood Sorrel

21C *Asclepias syriaca*
Common Milkweed

21D *Calystegia sepium*
Hedge Bindweed

21E *Clinopodium vulgare*
Wild Basil

21F *Dianthus deltoides*
Maiden Pink

22A *Leonurus cardiaca*
Motherwort

22B *Coronilla varia*
Crown Vetch

22C *Apocynum androsaemifolium*
Spreading Dogbane

22D *Asclepias incarnata*
Swamp Milkweed

22E *Centaurea maculosa*
Spotted Knapweed

22F *Desmodium glutinosum*
Clusterleaf Tick-trefoil

23A *Epilobium angustifolium*
Fireweed

23B *Platanthera psycodes*
Small Purple Fringed Orchid

23C *Trifolium pratense*
Red Clover

23D *Malva moschata*
Musk Mallow

23E *Saponaria officinalis*
Bouncing Bet

23F *Teucrium canadense*
American Germander

Purple to Blue

24 *Sisyrinchium montanum*
Common Blue-eyed Grass

25A *Hepatica americana*
Blunt-lobed Hepatica

25B *Glechoma hederacea*
Ground Ivy

25C *Hedyotis caerulea*
Bluets

25D *Geum rivale*
Water Avens

25E *Iris versicolor*
Large Blue Flag

25F *Geranium robertianum*
Herb Robert

26A *Veronica chamaedrys*
Bird's Eye Speedwell

26B *Erigeron pulchellus*
Robin's Plantain

26C *Mimulus ringens*
Monkey Flower

26D *Vicia cracca*
Cow Vetch

26E *Eupatorium maculatum*
Spotted Joe-Pye Weed

26F *Echium vulgare*
Viper's Bugloss

27A *Campanula rotundifolia*
Harebell

27B *Euphrasia officinalis*
Eyebright

27C *Myosotis scorpioides*
Forget-Me-Not

27D *Prunella vulgaris*
Selfheal

27E *Solanum dulcamara*
Climbing Nightshade

27F *Campanula rapunculoides*
Rover Bellflower

28A *Pontederia cordata*
Pickerel Weed

28B *Scutellaria galericulata*
Marsh Skullcap

28C *Verbena hastata*
Blue Vervain

28D *Arctium minus*
Common Burdock

28E *Cichorium intybus*
Chicory

28F *Cirsium arvense*
Canada Thistle

29A *Epipactis helleborine*
Helleborine

29B *Dipsacus sylvestris*
Teasel

29C *Lobelia inflata*
Indian Tobacco

29D *Monarda fistulosa*
Wild Bergamot

29E *Cirsium vulgare*
Bull Thistle

29F *Lobelia siphilitica*
Great Lobelia

30A *Lythrum salicaria*
Purple Loosestrife

30B *Thymus pulegioides*
Wild Thyme

30C *Aster cordifolius*
Heart-leaved Aster

30D *Aster novae-angliae*
New England Aster

30E *Gentiana clausa*
Closed Gentian

30F *Gentianopsis crinita*
Fringed Gentian

Green to Brown

31 *Arisaema triphyllum*
Jack-in-the-Pulpit

32A *Symplocarpus foetidus*
Skunk Cabbage

32B *Caulophyllum thalictroides*
Blue Cohosh

32C *Acorus calamus*
Sweet Flag

32D *Laportea canadensis*
Wood Nettle

32E *Urtica dioica*
Stinging Nettle

32F *Ambrosia artemisiifolia*
Ragweed

Pink to Red Flowers

Epigaea repens   April   Plate **19A**
Trailing Arbutus, Mayflower   Heath Family

Trailing arbutus is the state flower of Massachusetts. It is a low, spreading woody plant that may reach 2 feet tall. The 1/2-inch-wide, fragrant, pink or white flowers are tubular with 5 spreading lobes, and occur in terminal or axillary clusters. The leathery evergreen leaves are alternate, and are ovate, rounded, or heart shaped, and about 3 inches long. They have hairy margins.

The flowers are said to be edible in salads. Some American Indians and early settlers used the leaves to treat kidney stones and other ailments of the urinary system.

Trailing arbutus prefers exposed rocky sites or sandy woods. Plants are available commercially but are hard to cultivate and often fail when introduced into the garden. Keeping a purchased plant in a pot buried in the ground and moving it to a larger pot as the plant grows is said to increase success. Watch for trailing arbutus at Pleasant Valley Sanctuary, on Monument Mountain, and at Bartholomew's Cobble.

Claytonia caroliniana   April–May   Plate **19B**
Spring Beauty   Purslane Family

In early spring walks in the woods, watch for the delicate white to pink flowers of spring beauty. The flowers, 3/4 inch across, have 5 pink veined petals, occur in loose racemes of 2 to several flowers, only 1 or 2 of which are open at one time. When blooming, the plant is about 6 inches tall and has somewhat fleshy, opposite lanceolate leaves with distinct petioles. The leaves may be as long as 5 inches; only a single pair occurs on the flowering stem. The plant disappears by midsummer.

The leaves and flowers are edible and can be nibbled on while hiking. They have small potatolike tubers which taste bland and were once widely used by American Indians.

Spring beauty can be found, scattered about or in large patches, in open woods, especially in the northern part of our area. It is common on Mount Greylock.

Less common is the narrow-leaved spring beauty, *C. virginica*, which occurs in southern parts of our area. Look for it at Bartholomew's Cobble. This species has been found to develop chromosome abnormalities as it grows older and is used in studies of cell aging.

Trillium erectum   April–May   Plate **19C**
Red Trillium, Stinking Benjamin,
Wakerobin   Lily Family

Red trillium is easily recognized by its 3 maroon (rarely white or yellow), 2 1/2-inch petals on a solitary stalk over a whorl of 3 triangular to oval leaves. The leaves may be up to 8 inches long and the plant up to 16 inches tall. The single fruit is a 6-angled reddish berry, and the seeds are dispersed by ants.

The young leaves are edible, but picking them usually kills the plant. Historically, red trillium has been used to induce childbirth and to treat menstrual disorders and hemorrhages.

The plant is common and widely distributed in the

Berkshires. You will easily find it at Pleasant Valley Sanctuary, in Kennedy Park, at Notchview Reservation, on Mount Greylock, and at Bartholomew's Cobble, among other places.

Asarum canadense   April–June   Plate **19D**
Wild Ginger   Birthwort Family

Wild ginger is easily recognized by its large, heart-shaped leaves (3 to 5 inches across). The plant is seldom over 1 foot tall and may occur in small groups or large colonies. Look under the leaves to see the flowers, a maroon 3-lobed cup arising from between 2 leaves and close to or resting on the ground. As you explore the Berkshires, watch for variations in the form of the flowers and leaves. The lobes of the flowers are sometimes strongly reflexed, and the tips of the leaves vary from blunt to sharply pointed.

Wild ginger is pollinated by flies and beetles that visit the flowers, but it is probably mainly self-pollinated.

The rhizome tastes like true ginger and is edible. In colonial times it was ground and used as a spice or eaten candied. American Indians are reported to have used the root as a contraceptive and to promote menstruation. Recent research has found that the plant contains antimicrobial and antitumor substances.

Look for this species in moist wooded areas.

Aquilegia canadensis   May   Plate **19E**
Columbine   Buttercup Family

Columbine is an upright plant up to 2 feet tall found on cliffs and ledges, rocky areas, and moist ravines. The wiry stalks bear finely divided leaves ending in 3 leaflets about 1/2 inch wide. The solitary, nodding flowers consist of flaring red sepals and cylindrical yellow petals that end in long, slender, tubular spurs containing nectar. Long yellow stamens dangle below the flower.

Columbine is pollinated by moths, bees, and hummingbirds. Bumblebees, which can't reach the nectar through the open end of the petals, bite holes in the tips of the spurs to obtain it. The 5-parted seed capsule is held upright and splits open when dry to scatter the small, shiny black seeds when swayed by the wind.

Some American Indians chewed the seeds to relieve headaches, but all parts of the plant are potentially poisonous. This species is widely cultivated as a garden plant; yellow and double forms are available.

Look for columbine in woods along trails. Good displays can be found at Bartholomew's Cobble and along the Taconic Parkway in New York State.

Cardamine pratensis   May–June   Plate **19F**
Cuckoo Flower   Mustard Family

Cuckoo flower is identified as a member of the mustard family by its 4-petaled flowers. The 3/4-inch flowers may be pink or white, and occur in terminal clusters on erect unbranched stems which may grow to 1 1/2 feet tall. The leaves are pinnately compound; those in the basal rosette have round leaflets while the stem leaves are alternate with narrow leaflets.

The pink- to purple-flowered form, which was introduced from Europe, is commonly found in wet areas in lawns, meadows, and along roadsides, often in dense colonies. The white-flowered form is native to the Berkshires and occurs in wet areas such as bogs and swamps, usually as single plants. The native form is threatened in Massachusetts.

Cuckoo flower is widely grown as an ornamental; double-flowered varieties are available.

Cypripedium acaule   May–June   Plate **20A**
Pink Lady's Slipper, Moccasin Flower   Orchis Family
Lady's slippers are immediately recognized by their greatly inflated lower petal, the "slipper." This species is the lady's slipper you are most likely to find in our area. The slipper is pink (as you go north, flowers tend to be less intensely colored, and white flowers are often found), with a distinct furrow running down the middle. Two narrow, brownish petals arise from the base of the pouch as do 2 green bracts (the lower bract is actually 2 fused together). The flower is held on a leafless stem up to 18 inches high above 2 large oval, light green, basal leaves. The leaves are often evergreen, and you can thus recognize the plant throughout the year. This is the only species of lady's slipper in our area without stem leaves.

This and other lady's slippers are pollinated by bees, which get neither nectar nor pollen for their efforts. The flower attract them with fragrance and then acts as a trap from which the bee can escape only by brushing past the stamens and pistil.

The species is found on acid soil in wet and dry woods and in bogs. It often occurs on the spongy mats of vegetation that overgrow rocks. Although it often colonizes disturbed areas, it is almost impossible to transplant into gardens probably because the plant relies on a mycorrhizal fungus that seldom survives in cultivation. All plants offered for sale have been taken from the wild and probably will not survive long.

American Indians used the plant to treat nervous diseases, and it was used in the 19th century as a sedative. It causes contact dermatitis in some people.

Keep your eyes open for pink lady's slippers on Mount Greylock and October Mountain, at Pleasant Valley Sanctuary, and in Beartown Forest.

Geranium maculatum   May–June   Plate **20B**
Wild Geranium, Cranesbill   Geranium Family

A showy 2-foot-high mound covered with rose pink 1 1/2-inch solitary flowers in the spring is likely to be this species. The beauty of wild geranium rivals that of many cultivated flowers. The terminal flowers have 5 petals and later develop into the long, pointed fruit which resembles a crane's bill. When the fruit dries, the 5 segments suddenly spring upward, catapulting the large seeds some distance from the mother plant. The leaves are opposite and have 5 palmate lobes.

The root was once used as an astringent to stop bleeding.

Wild geranium prefers shaded areas in woods. It can be found along most trails and roads in our area.

Pedicularis canadensis   May–June   Plate **20C**
Wood Betony, Lousewort   Figwort Family

Wood betony looks like a fuzzy fern with flowers. The flowers are irregular with 2 lips, the upper hoodlike and the lower 3-lobed. The 3/4-inch flowers are either red, usually with yellow at the base, or entirely yellow and occur in dense terminal clusters. The deeply pinnately dissected alternate leaves resemble hairy fern fronds; they may be up to 5 inches long. The erect, hairy stems occur in clusters and may reach 16 inches in height.

A parasite on other plants, wood betony is found along woodland borders and in clearings. American Indians made a root tea to treat a variety of ailments. Some tribes added finely grated roots to food as an aphrodisiac.

A large patch of this species occurs at Bash Bish Falls on the hillside opposite the steps to the base of the falls.

Polygala paucifolia   May–June   Plate **18**
Fringed Polygala, Gay Wings   Milkwort Family
Fringed polygala is often mistaken for an orchid. If you find a large patch of what looks like a small pink orchid, look carefully as it may be this species. The flowers are pink or rose with 3 petals which are fringed with yellow or rose at their tips and together form a tube about 3/4 inch long. There are 5 sepals: 2 larger ones which are pink and petallike and are held above the petals to form wings, and 3 smaller, lower green ones. There may be 1 to 4 flowers arising from the leaf axils. The 2 1/2-inch, oval, evergreen leaves are alternate and crowded into a cluster at the top of the plant. There are also a few scalelike leaves on the stem, which may reach 6 inches tall. The plant also produces nonopening, self-pollinating flowers in the summer and fall.

It was once believed that eating plants of this genus increased milk production in humans and cows. A related species, Seneca snakeroot, *P. senega*, was used by the Seneca Indians to treat snakebite. Although recorded from the Berkshires, Seneca snakeroot has not been found in this area in recent years.

Watch for fringed polygala at Bartholomew's Cobble and on Mount Everett.

Streptopus roseus   May–June   Plate **20D**
Rose Twisted Stalk, Rosybells   Lily Family
    The flowers of rose twisted stalk are pink to purple nodding bells with 6 flaring segments hanging on short, twisted stalks in the leaf axils. The plant can be single or branched and has a shrubby appearance. The lanceolate leaves are arranged alternately and sessile on the zig-zaggy stem. The plant is a foot or 2 tall.
    The red berries are edible but, like those of related plants, are cathartic and thus should be eaten in small amounts.
    Rose twisted stalk is found in moist woods. Watch for it on Mount Greylock.

Hesperis matronalis   May–July   Plate **20E**
Dame's Rocket, Sweet Rocket   Mustard Family
    In summer, you will often find large, conspicuous stands of pink, purple, or white flowers which resemble garden phlox, *Phlox paniculata*. If the flowers are about 1 inch wide and have 4 petals, you have probably found dame's rocket. The flowers occur in terminal clusters and are fragrant, especially in the evening. The leaves are lanceolate, pointed, toothed, and sessile or short-stalked. They are covered with soft hairs and alternate on the stems, which may reach 4 feet tall.
    An introduction from Eurasia, dame's rocket was once used as a diuretic and to induce sweating.
    It is frequent along roadsides and fence rows, on old home sites, and in waste areas.

Lychnis flos-cuculi   June   Plate **20F**
Ragged Robin, Cuckoo Flower   Pink Family

Watch for a delicate wash of pink in meadows to find this species. The flowers occur in open panicles and have 5 pink petals which are deeply dissected, giving them a ragged appearance. The plant has 4 or 5 pairs of opposite narrow, lance-shaped leaves and stands about 2 feet tall.

Ragged robin forms dense colonies in moist meadows. It makes a wonderful display each year along Rte. 183 between the Rockwell Museum and the Berkshire Botanical Garden, where it is also cultivated. Ragged robin was introduced from Europe.

Sarracenia purpurea   June   Plate **21A**
Pitcher Plant   Pitcher Plant Family

The flowers and leaves of the pitcher plant are unlike those of any other plant that grows in the Berkshires. The nodding flowers are dark red, about 2 1/2 inches wide, on leafless stems a foot or more tall. They have 5 petals and a 5-pointed umbrella-shaped style. The purple-veined evergreen leaves are basal and pitcher-shaped. Each leaf bears a wing along one side and a bristly hood; leaves may be as long as 12 inches. The leaves are often filled with water and serve as insect traps; hairs inside the leaf make it easy for an insect to move downward but difficult to climb out. If the insect falls into the water, it is digested by enzymes secreted from the leaves. Some insects have evolved resistance to the enzymes and their larvae inhabit the leaves, feeding on bacteria which occur in the water.

The roots of pitcher plant have been used to treat upset stomach and constipation. Some American

Indians believed that the root could be used to prevent smallpox.

Pitcher plants occur in bogs and peaty soils on October Mountain and in Savoy State Forest.

Oxalis acetosella   June–July   Plate **21B**
Wood Sorrel, Wood Shamrock   Wood Sorrel Family
A low-growing plant (up to 6 inches tall) with white or pink flowers and cloverlike leaves found in a shady woodland is likely to be this species. The solitary, 3/4 inch flowers have 5 notched petals with dark pink veins. The basal leaves have long stems and 3 heart-shaped leaflets. The flowers and leaves close at night and in deep shade. Wood sorrel also produces underground flowers which do not open and produce seeds without being pollinated.

The sour leaves are edible as a trail nibble or can be brewed into a tea. This species was used as a culinary herb in Elizabethan England. Seed decoctions have also been taken to treat spermatorrhea (flow of semen without sexual stimulation). The plant contains oxalates and is potentially toxic in large quantities; it is known to have killed sheep.

Watch for it in moist woods at Bartholomew's Cobble, at Notchview Reservation, on Mount Greylock, and along the Appalachian Trail.

Asclepias syriaca   June–August   Plate **21C**
Common Milkweed, Silkweed   Milkweed Family
Milkweeds are easily identified by their distinctive flowers which look like miniature versions of the stone lanterns often seen in Oriental gardens topped by a little

5-pointed crown. The fragrant flowers of common milk-weed occur in round terminal and axillary drooping umbels 2 to 4 inches wide. The color of the flowers is quite variable, ranging from greenish to brownish purple. The large (4- to 11-inch) oblong to oval leaves are arranged oppositely on erect, unbranched stems. The entire plant is somewhat downy. The seedpods are elongate with pointed tips and have a warty surface. The mature seeds are endowed with numerous silky hairs and are dispersed by the wind. Milkweeds have milky sap. (See also swamp milkweed, p. 81.)

Common milkweed is the major food plant of the monarch butterfly, *Danaus plexippus*, in the Northeast. The plant contains cardiac glycosides which are absorbed by the larvae and retained by the adult butterflies. These substances are toxic to birds, which after one taste of a monarch learn to avoid them. The bright color of the monarch is thought to be a warning sign to potential predators. The viceroy butterfly, *Limenitis archippus*, which closely resembles the monarch, does not feed on milkweed, but is believed to gain protection from predators by mimicking the monarch.

Although poisonous raw, young milkweed shoots less than 8 inches tall and pods less than 1 inch long can be eaten if boiled in a couple of changes of water to remove the bitter taste. Take care not to confuse young milkweeds with the similar poisonous dogbanes which also have milky sap, but are branched and lack hairs. American Indians used the milky sap to treat skin ailments. The silk from the seedpods has been used to stuff pillows and feather beds, and during World War II was used to stuff life jackets. The dried pods can be used in dried arrangements. The stem fibers are strong, soft, and flexible, and are used by spinners and basketmakers.

Calystegia sepium   June–August   Plate **21D**
Hedge Bindweed   Morning Glory Family

Watch for a plant that looks like a pink or white morning glory with flowers up to 3 inches long. The flowers are funnel shaped and occur singly at the ends of long axillary stems. The alternate leaves are arrow shaped with blunt basal lobes. The stems may be as long as 10 feet and trail on the ground or twine over other plants. The flowers open in the morning and close in the afternoon.

Hedge bindweed has been traditionally used to treat jaundice, and the root was once used as a purgative.

This and related species are hard-to-control weeds and are frequently seen along roadsides and in cultivated fields.

Clinopodium vulgare   June–August   Plate **21E**
Wild Basil, Dogmint   Mint Family

The pink purple flowers of wild basil occur in dense, rounded terminal or upper axillary clusters. They are about 1/2 inch long and are mingled with many hairy bracts. The corolla is 2-lipped with the upper lip notched and the lower 3-lobed. The leaves are opposite, oval, and slightly lobed, and may be up to 1 1/2 inches long. The stem is square, hairy, and often branched.

The leaves of wild basil can be used to make a tea or used like garden basil, but are not as highly flavored.

Watch for it in old fields, in meadows, and along trails and roadsides. It is common along the trails in Kennedy Park.

Dianthus deltoides   June–August   Plate **21F**
Maiden Pink   Pink Family

Watch for pink to red purple, almost fluorescent flowers in dry fields and along trails and roadsides. The 1/2- to 3/4-inch-wide flowers have 5 toothed petals and a distinct dark ring near their centers. They occur solitarily on erect, unbranched stems which may reach 1 1/2 feet tall. The leaves are opposite, light green, and grasslike, and are to 1 inch long.

The fields adjoining the rest stop on Rte. 7 in Sheffield are solid pink with maiden pinks in early summer. Maiden pinks are widely cultivated as a ground cover and are available in many named varieties. A similar species, *D. armeria*, Deptford pink, is also found in the Berkshires. Its flowers lack the dark central ring and are dotted with white. The stems are usually branched, and the flowers occur in small clusters.

Leonurus cardiaca   June–August   Plate **22A**
Motherwort   Mint Family

Motherwort has pink to purple 2-lipped flowers, about 1/2 inch long. The lips are bearded or furry, and the calyx lobes are spiny. The flowers occur in dense, whorled clusters in the upper leaf axils. The plant has a basal rosette of evergreen leaves and opposite, palmately divided stem leaves with 3 lobes. The leaves have sharp teeth and are aromatic. The stem is square, sometimes branched, and may reach 4 feet tall.

The dried top and leaves have been used to treat menstruation and to aid in childbirth; a leaf tonic was used to treat heart ailments and hysteria. The plant is an alternate host for cucumber mosaic disease.

Motherwort is introduced from Europe and occurs

on roadsides and in fields and gardens. It is quite common at Bartholomew's Cobble around the parking lot.

Coronilla varia   June–September   Plate **22B**
Crown Vetch, Axseed   Pea Family
    Pink to white pealike flowers in umbels of 10 to 15 on single erect axillary stems identify this species. The plants sprawl on the ground or over other vegetation. The leaves are alternate and pinnately compound with 10 to 25 leaflets.
    Crown vetch was introduced from Europe, where it is cultivated for hay. It is widely used to stabilize soil on roadsides and as an ornamental ground cover. The seeds are said to be poisonous.

Apocynum androsaemifolium   July   Plate **22C**
Spreading Dogbane, Wild Ipecac   Dogbane Family
    Spreading dogbane is a somewhat shrubby plant with 1/3-inch bell-shaped, nodding flowers in axillary or terminal clusters. The flowers are pink, with distinct stripes on the inside, and have 5 recurved lobes. The leaves are opposite, stalked, and droopy; they are hairy underneath. The stem is smooth and branched, and the plant has milky sap.
    Spreading dogbane contains cymarin, a cardioactive glycoside, which acts much like digitalis. American Indians used this species for a heart medicine. It was once used to treat dropsy (edema), was also used in the 19th century to promote sweating and as an expectorant, and has been shown to have antitumor activity. The plant is poisonous and is reported to have killed livestock. American Indians twisted the bark to make

thread and bow strings.

Spreading dogbane is found in open areas such as meadows, wood edges, and roadsides. There is a large stand of it in the field east of the Colonel Ashley House.

Asclepias incarnata   July–August   Plate **22D**
Swamp Milkweed   Milkweed Family

A plant with pink to rose flowers similar to those of common milkweed, *A. syriaca* (see the entry for common milkweed, p. 76, for a detailed description), is probably swamp milkweed. The flowers are about 1/4 inch long and occur in terminal umbels. The leaves are opposite, lanceolate to oblong, tapering at the tips, and up to 4 inches long. The stems are erect, frequently branched, and up to 5 feet tall. This species has milky juice.

Herbalists use the roots to induce vomiting, promote urination, and treat intestinal parasites.

Swamp milkweed occurs in wet areas in woods, meadows, and on the margins of water bodies. It can be found at Pleasant Valley Sanctuary, in Kennedy Park, and at Bartholomew's Cobble. There is a cultivated form with white flowers.

Centaurea maculosa   July–August   Plate **22E**
Spotted Knapweed   Aster Family

Spotted knapweed resembles a pink or lavender version of the commonly grown bachelor's button, *C. cyanus*. The 1-inch-wide thistlelike flower heads consist of only disk flowers and have prickly, black-tipped bracts. The heads are terminal or occur in the leaf axils of the wiry, hairy, much-branched stems, which may reach 3 feet tall. The highly dissected leaves are 4 to 8 inches long.

Spotted knapweed was introduced from Europe and is found on dry sites in open fields, along roadsides, and in waste areas. A similar plant, brown knapweed, *C. jacea*, also occurs in the Berkshires. It has toothed rather than finely dissected leaves.

Desmodium glutinosum   July–August Plate **22F**
Clusterleaf Tick-trefoil   Pea Family
 Six (or possibly seven) species of tick-trefoil occur in the Berkshires. They all have 1/4- to 1/2-inch long, pealike pink to purple flowers and leaves palmately divided into 3 leaflets. One species, *D. rotundifolium*, low tick-trefoil, is a vine with roundish leaves. The other species grow erect. All produce fruit resembling fuzzy pea pods that easily break into triangular, single-seeded segments called loments. These are covered with tiny, hooked spines and cling to fur and clothing. Almost anyone who hikes in the woods has had occasion to pick these "ticks" from socks or pants.
 Clusterleaf tick-trefoil is distinguished by having a whorl of leaves at the base of the flower stalk, whereas the leaves of the other species are arranged alternately along the stalks.
 Tick-trefoils usually occur in woodlands in open areas and along trails and roads. They are widely distributed in the Berkshires.
 Several species have been used in folk medicine to reduce fever and to treat dysentery and liver diseases.

Epilobium angustifolium   July–August Plate **23A**
Fireweed, Willow Herb   Evening Primrose Family
 Fireweed is so called because it is among the first

plants to recolonize burnt areas. The flowers occur in showy elongated terminal spikes which may have buds at the top and seedpods at the bottom. The flowers are pink, rarely white, 1 to 1 1/2 inches wide with 4 unequal clawed petals. The leaves are alternate, lanceolate, narrow and willowlike, up to 8 inches long, with pointed tips and conspicuous veins. The smooth and often reddish stems may reach 6 1/2 feet tall.

The young shoots may be eaten like asparagus, the leaves as a potherb, and the flower buds in salads. Some American Indians used the pith to make soup. In Russia, the leaves are dried and used to make kaporie tea. The plant was once used to treat respiratory problems. It is used in perennial borders, and several cultivars are available.

Fireweed is an early successional species and may be found on recently cleared land, burned areas, and open fields. It can be found on Mount Greylock.

Platanthera psycodes   July–August   Plate **23B**
Small Purple Fringed Orchid   Orchis Family

It is always a treat to find a purple fringed orchid. Keep your eyes open for a plant 1 to 3 feet tall with a cylindrical terminal raceme of rose purple flowers. Then check for a 3-parted lower lip with a distinct fringe. The flowers are fragrant and usually slightly cocked to one side. The leaves are alternate, lanceolate to oval, and sheath the stem. Purple fringed orchids are pollinated by moths.

There are two species of purple fringed orchid. The smaller, small purple fringed orchid, *P. psycodes*, is the more common in the Berkshires. It has a flower cluster less than 2 inches wide and blooms two to three weeks later than the larger species, large purple fringed orchid, *P. grandiflora*. The latter has a flower cluster more than 2 inches wide. Both forms may be found on Mount Greylock; the smaller has been recorded at Bartholomew's Cobble.

Trifolium pratense   July–August   Plate **23C**
Red Clover   Pea Family

In mid- to late summer roadsides and fields will be rosy with the blossoms of red clover. The pealike flowers are about 1/2 inch long and occur in dense, globular heads about 1 inch wide. The leaves are alternate, palmately divided into 3 leaflets, and held on long stalks. Each leaflet has a whitish V-shaped mark across its center. The stem is hairy and erect, growing to 2 feet tall.

The young flowers and leaves may be added to a salad or cooked as greens. Dried flower heads are sometimes added to other teas, and the heads and seeds can be ground and used as a flour substitute. Red clover tea is used in folk medicine for sore throats and colds. The flowers were once smoked in antiasthma cigarettes. The plant was once regarded as protection from witchcraft and evil spirits.

Red clover is the second most important forage legume in the United States and is often planted as a soil-improving crop and as a nectar source for honeybees. The seeds and foliage are eaten by birds and mammals, especially ruffed grouse, cottontail rabbits, and woodchucks.

An introduction from Europe, red clover is the state flower of Vermont and is found throughout the Northeast.

Alsike clover, *T. hybridum*, is also found in and near

cultivated areas in the Berkshires. It has white flowers with a pinkish cast and lacks the V-shaped marks on the leaflets.

Malva moschata   July–September   Plate **23D**
Musk Mallow   Mallow Family

Musk mallow might remind you of hollyhocks. The flowers are pink to white, up to 2 inches wide, and consist of 5 slightly notched, wedge-shaped petals surrounding a central column. (This structure, a distinctive feature of the mallow family, comprises filaments that are united into a tube around the style.) The flowers are terminal and axial and have a faint odor of musk. The stem leaves are alternate and deeply palmately lobed while the basal leaves are 5-lobed. The stems are hairy and may reach 3 feet tall.

Because of their high mucilage content, the young leaves are sometimes used to thicken soups. The seeds may be eaten as a trail snack or added to salads. This and related species are sometimes used in cough remedies. The species is often grown as an ornamental, but it self-seeds readily and may become a pest.

An introduction from Europe, musk mallow is commonly found in disturbed fields and along roadsides.

Saponaria officinalis   July–October   Plate **23E**
Bouncing Bet, Soapwort   Pink Family

Bouncing bet has pale pink or white flowers with 5 notched petals enclosed by a narrow tube formed by the fused sepals borne in a crowded terminal cyme. Plants may be up to 2 1/2 feet tall, with stems swollen at the nodes and opposite oval-lanceolate leaves with prominent veins. The flowers are fragrant and remain open at night when they are visited by hawk moths.

Bouncing bet is an old name for a washerwoman and refers to the use of this plant as a soap substitute. If bits of the plant are rubbed together between wet hands, soaplike suds are formed. It is still used by museums for cleaning old tapestries. The Pennsylvania Dutch used bouncing bet to give a foamy head to beer. The foaming action is due to compounds called saponins, varieties of which are used in modern brewing.

This species is introduced from the Old World and is common along roads and in fields. It is also cultivated, and a double form can occasionally be found in the wild.

Teucrium canadense   August–September   Plate **23F**
American Germander, Wood Sage   Mint Family

A 3-foot upright plant with a terminal spike of pink to pale purple flowers may be American germander. The flowers are irregular with a prominent lower lip and stamens projecting through a cleft in the small upper lip. The leaves are lanceolate, toothed, up to 5 inches long, and hairy underneath; they are arranged oppositely on the hairy square stem.

American germander was traditionally used to make a tea to induce menstruation, urination, or sweating.

Watch for this species in moist, shady areas such as woods, thickets, and shorelines. It is quite common near the parking lot at Bartholomew's Cobble and in nearby open areas.

Purple to Blue Flowers

Hepatica   April   Plate **25A**
Hepatica, Liver Leaf   Buttercup Family
The flowers of the hepaticas appear in early spring before the new leaves are fully unfurled. They have 6 to 12 petallike sepals which may be white, pink, or bluish lavender. The evergreen basal leaves have 3 lobes and hairy stems. Two species of hepatica are found in the Berkshires. Sharp-leaved hepatica, *H. acutifolia*, has pointed leaf lobes and occurs on moist limestone areas; blunt-lobed hepatica, *H. americana*, has rounded leaf lobes and occurs in acid to neutral dry woods. Hybrids occur where the two species grow close together.

The leaf is said to resemble a liver in shape and color and, following the doctrine of signatures, which claimed that a plant could cure ailments of a body part that it resembled, was once used to treat liver problems. Although no scientific justification has been found for such use, hepaticas were widely used in the 19th century for patent medicine liver tonics.

Both species of hepatica are widely distributed in our area.

Glechoma hederacea   April–July   Plate **25B**
Ground Ivy, Creeping Charlie   Mint Family
Anyone who tends a lawn or garden in the Berkshires knows this plant, which spreads rapidly to form dense mats in any unoccupied patch of ground. The flowers

are blue to violet, about 3/4 inch long, 2-lipped, and occur in axillary clusters of 3 to 7. The flower's upper lip is 2-lobed and the lower, 3-lobed. The distinctive round to kidney-shaped scalloped evergreen leaves are up to 1 1/2 inches wide, opposite, and aromatic. The stem is square and trailing, rooting at the nodes.

The plant was once used to clarify beer. In the 19th century, the dried leaves were used to make a tea to treat lung ailments and lead poisoning. Horses are occasionally poisoned by eating large quantities of this plant.

An introduction from Europe, ground ivy is found in lawns, gardens, moist woods, and shady open spaces. Just look down; it's probably there.

Hedyotis caerulea   April–July   Plate **25C**
Bluets, Quaker Ladies   Madder (Bedstraw) Family

Bluets often form clumps of pale blue flowers in lawns or damp fields. The 1/2-inch flowers are tubular and 4-lobed with yellow centers. Each is solitary on the end of a wiry stem, a characteristic that distinguishes them from forget-me-nots (see *Myosotis scorpioides*, p. 96). The leaves are spatula shaped, opposite on the stems, and in basal rosettes where they are about 1/2 inch long. Usually the stems are unbranched and may reach 8 inches tall.

Some American Indians brewed a tea from the leaves to treat bed-wetting. Bluets are often grown in rock gardens.

Look for them throughout the Berkshires in damp open areas.

Geum rivale   May–June   Plate **25D**
Water Avens, Purple Avens   Rose Family

Water avens often appears as a purplish haze in the middle of a damp field where it might be mistaken for flowering grasses. Up close, you will find that the 1/2-inch globular nodding flowers which often occur in threes have purple sepals and yellowish petals. The alternate stem leaves are 3-parted with toothed leaflets; the basal leaves are divided into many segments with the terminal one about 1 inch long. The plant may reach 2 or 3 feet in height.

The root can be used to make a beverage that is said to taste like hot chocolate. Tea made from the foliage has been used as a diuretic.

Water avens requires moist to wet soil and is found in low areas in fields, in bogs, and near water. Look for it at Pleasant Valley Sanctuary, in Kennedy Park, and at Field Farm Reservation.

Iris versicolor   May–June   Plate **25E**
Large Blue Flag, Wild Iris   Iris Family

This is the only native iris in the Berkshires; any blue iris you find in the wild is this species. The plant has 1 to several terminal 2- to 4-inch violet blue flowers and narrow, swordlike leaves up to 3 feet tall.

All parts of the plant are poisonous and have been reported to kill livestock. The colonists used the dried rhizome as a cathartic and diuretic, and it has been used homeopathically to treat migraines. The species is commonly cultivated; reddish and pink selections are available.

Large blue flag prefers wet areas and is common in marshes, bogs, wet fields, ditches, and along ponds.

Look for it on October Mountain, at Bartholomew's Cobble, Pleasant Valley Sanctuary, and Mill Pond.

The yellow flag, *I. pseudacorus,* is an introduced species that is found around many ponds in our area. It blooms in midsummer. A large stand of it can be seen to the east from Rte. 7 on the north edge of Great Barrington.

Sisyrinchium montanum   May–June   Plate **24**
Common Blue-eyed Grass   Iris Family

This and related species are usually found as 3/4-inch purplish blue flowers among grasses. The flowers have 6 bristle-tipped tepals and a yellow center. They occur singly or in small terminal clusters and are over-topped by a pointed bract. The leaves are basal, grass-like, and more than half as tall as the plant; the stem is unbranched and flattened or winged and up to 1 1/2 feet tall.

Some American Indians used this and similar species as a laxative.

Common blue-eyed grass is found in sunny open fields and meadows. Three other species of *Sisyrinchium* are found in the Berkshires. Slender blue-eyed grass, *S. mucronatum*, has a sharp bract over the flowers, a very slender, barely winged stem, and leaves only about half as tall as the flowering stem. In the other two species, the flowering stem has a bract in the middle of the plant from which the flowers arise. In this case, there is no sharp-pointed bract above the flowers. Stout blue-eyed grass, *S. angustifolium*, has a distinctly winged lower stem more than 1/8 inch wide. Eastern blue-eyed grass, *S. atlanticum*, has a barely winged lower stem less than 1/8 inch wide. The common and stout species can be found at Pleasant Valley Sanctuary; stout blue-eyed grass also grows at Bartholomew's Cobble. Several species are cultivated as rock garden plants.

Geranium robertianum   May–August   Plate **25F**
Herb Robert   Geranium Family

A sprawling plant with 1/2-inch pinkish purple flowers is likely to be herb Robert. The flowers have 5 petals and occur in pairs in the upper leaf axils. The foliage is dark green with a reddish tint. The opposite leaves are palmately divided into 3 to 5 pinnately divided leaflets. The terminal leaflet is usually stalked. The stems are hairy and sticky and highly branched, and the plant may reach 2 feet tall. The plant has a disagreeable odor if bruised.

The plant has been used as an astringent to treat skin irritations and also used to relieve diarrhea and other digestive disorders. It is often planted as an ornamental, and white and double varieties have been cultivated.

Herb Robert is an annual of moist areas in woods and along roadsides, often in weepy areas on rock ledges. Watch for it at Bartholomew's Cobble, Pleasant Valley Sanctuary, and at Canoe Meadows.

Veronica chamaedrys   May–September   Plate **26A**
Bird's Eye Speedwell   Figwort Family

Bird's eye speedwell has 1/2-inch-wide, 4-lobed blue flowers in which the lower lobe is noticeably smaller in clusters up to 6 inches long arising from the leaf axils. The opposite leaves are oval, toothed, and up to 1 inch long. The hairy stems are prostrate, rooting at the nodes, with erect branches that may reach 16 inches tall.

This species is introduced from Europe and is found in lawns, gardens, and other disturbed areas.

The dried leaves are used to make a tea.

Eleven species of *Veronica* have been reported in the Berkshires. One is an erect garden escape, the others more or less sprawling, creeping, or prostrate plants. All have the distinctive 4-lobed flowers with a smaller lower lobe which are either blue or white with blue markings. Six of the species have been introduced from Europe or Asia.

Several species of speedwells can be found commonly in lawns, others in damp areas.

Erigeron pulchellus   June   Plate **26B**
Robin's Plantain   Aster Family

Robin's plantain is one of the earliest of the asterlike flowers to bloom and one of the showiest of the native fleabanes. The flower heads are 1 to 1 1/2 inches across with violet to white rays and yellow disks. The heads occur either solitarily or in small terminal branched clusters (corymbs). The toothed leaves are ovate to lanceolate and occur mostly in basal rosettes; the few on the stem are alternate. The plant is soft and hairy and may reach 2 feet tall. It spreads by rhizomes and may form dense colonies. This species is highly attractive to bees and butterflies.

Robin's plantain is found throughout the Berkshires in fields and open woods, usually in light shade. It is often grown in woodland gardens, but tends to become weedy in rich soils.

Mimulus ringens   June–July   Plate **26C**
Monkey Flower   Figwort Family
The flowers of monkey flower, said to resemble the face of a monkey, are blue to purple; 2-lipped, with the upper lip 2-lobed and the lower 3-lobed; about 1 inch long; and are borne on stalks in the leaf axils. The opposite leaves are lanceolate, finely toothed, and sessile, and sometimes clasp the stem. The smooth stem is square in cross section, and the plant may grow to about 3 1/2 feet tall.

Monkey flower is found in wet areas on shorelines, in swamps, and roadside ditches. Some western American Indians used the young leaves and stems as salad greens. Early cowboys made a poultice of the plant to treat rope burns.

Good places to see monkey flower are Pleasant Valley Sanctuary, Bartholomew's Cobble, and the state wildlife management areas along the Housatonic River in Pittsfield and Lenox.

Vicia cracca   June–July   Plate **26D**
Bitter Vetch, Cow Vetch   Pea Family
Blue to purplish 1/2-inch-long pealike flowers in crowded axial clusters of 9 to 30 flowers indicate this species. The leaves are alternate, pinnately compound, and terminate in a tendril. Each leaf has 5 to 12 pairs of 1-inch gray green leaflets with pointed tips. The stem is thin and sprawling or climbing to 3 1/2 feet long. The stem has inconspicuous hairs held flat against it. The very similar hairy vetch, *V. villosa*, has distinct spreading hairs on the stems.

Bitter vetch is used as a cover crop and to stabilize sandy soils. It is found throughout the Berkshires on roadsides and in fields and meadows.

Eupatorium maculatum   June–August   Plate **26E**
Spotted Joe-Pye Weed   Aster Family
    The Joe-Pye weeds are among the dominant elements of the flora of late summer to early fall. They are tall, robust plants with large, flat-topped, fuzzy clusters of pinkish purple flowers. Three species are found in the Berkshires.

    The individual flower heads of spotted Joe-Pye weed are about 1/2 inch wide and consist entirely of disk flowers. The leaves are in whorls of 4 or 5, lanceolate tapering at both ends, coarsely toothed, and up to 8 inches long. The stems are purple or spotted with purple, and the plants may be up to 6 feet tall.

    Spotted Joe-Pye weed is found in damp areas along roadsides, in meadows, and along water bodies.

    The origin of the name is unclear. Some say it was named after an American Indian herb doctor in the Massachusetts Bay Colony who used this or related plants to treat typhus. Others say it's named after a 19th-century "Indian theme promoter."

    Species of Joe-Pye weed have been used as a diuretic, as a tea to treat fever and chills, for sore uterus after childbirth, and as a wash for rheumatism.

    Sweet Joe-Pye weed, *E. purpureum*, smells like vanilla when bruised, has fewer flowers per head, and has green stems with purple only at the nodes. Hollowstem Joe-Pye weed, *E. fistulosum*, has a hollow stem covered with a slight bloom.

    Joe-Pye weeds are common throughout the Berkshires.

Echium vulgare   June–August   Plate **26F**
Viper's Bugloss, Blue Devil   Borage Family

A hairy, bristly plant with bright blue, 3/4-inch flowers is likely to be viper's bugloss. The corolla is funnel-shaped and 5-lobed; protruding stamens have red filaments. The flowers occur in dense, coiled, 1-sided clusters in the upper leaf axils. The flowers open one at a time. At first, the plant appears to have a neat terminal spike, but as the individual coiled clusters open, the plant becomes quite straggly. The oblong to lanceolate leaves are alternate on the stem and also form a basal rosette. The entire plant is often dotted with red.

The dried leaves have been used as a diuretic. Prolonged use as a tea can lead to Budd-Chiari syndrome, a liver disease. The plant contains pyrrolizidine and has caused death in cattle. It may cause contact dermatitis if handled. According to the doctrine of signatures, the plant was used to treat snakebite because markings on the stem were thought to resemble snakes.

This introduction from Europe is common in dry areas along roads, in fields, and in waste areas.

Campanula rotundifolia   June–September   Plate **27A**
Harebell, Bluebells of Scotland   Bellflower Family

Harebells are airy plants with 1-inch-long, 5-lobed violet blue flowers nodding singly or in small clusters from wiry stems. The basal leaves are round but are usually withered by the time the plant flowers. The stem leaves are alternate, narrow, and up to 4 inches long. The stems are smooth and slender to 1 1/2 feet tall.

Harebells are found in meadows and dry, open fields, and on rocky slopes. They are easy to find at Bartholomew's Cobble. This species has many geographic forms in the Northern Hemisphere and is widely cultivated.

Euphrasia officinalis   June–September   Plate **27B**
Eyebright   Figwort Family
     Eyebright resembles a small mint, but it has a round stem and the leaves are not aromatic. The 1/3-inch lavender to white flowers are marked with distinct purple lines, and the lower lip has 3 notched lobes. The flowers occur in spikelike terminal clusters. The leaves are opposite and ovate, with coarse, bristly teeth. They may be up to 3/4 inch long. The stems are hairy and about 1 foot tall. Eyebright is a semiparasite on grasses.
     It was used as a folk remedy for eye ailments, especially conjunctivitis.
     Watch for eyebright on roadsides and fields. It can be found on Mount Greylock and along the entrance road to Notchview Reservation.

Myosotis scorpioides   June–September   Plate **27C**
Forget-Me-Not   Borage Family
     The bright sky blue flowers of forget-me-nots are a common sight in the Berkshires. The 1/2-inch, 5-lobed, funnel-shaped flowers have a yellow center, or eye, and occur on coiled branches that unroll as the flowers open. The leaves are alternate, oblate, and up to 3 inches long. The stem is sprawling, with erect tips, and may reach 2 feet long. The entire plant is hairy. (Compare bluets, p. 88.)
     According to German folklore, a knight who had fallen into a flooded stream flung a cluster of this plant to his damsel on shore, entreating "Forget me not!" as he was swept away.

Forget-me-nots were introduced from Europe and can now be found in damp areas throughout the Berkshires. They are the state flower of Alaska.

Two other species of forget-me-not can be found in the Berkshires. A native species, wild forget-me-not, *M. laxa*, has tiny flowers less than 1/4 inch wide, and also blooms from June through September. Since the flowers are so small the plant is not showy and is easily overlooked. It is common in lightly shaded wet areas but may also be found in urban yards. The garden forget-me-not, *M. sylvatica*, is more showy than the other two species and tends to bloom mostly in May. It forms small mounds of 1/2-inch flowers and has less hairy stems than the other two species. It is usually found around dwellings and is abundant at the Berkshire Botanical Garden in spring. White or pink flowers occur occasionally in all the species. Many species and varieties of forget-me-nots are cultivated.

Prunella vulgaris　　　　June–September　　Plate **27D**
Selfheal, Heal-all　　　　　　　　　　Mint Family

Watch for short cylinders of purple, 2-lipped flowers (the upper lip forming a hood over the fringed lower one) on sprawling stems with square stems and ovate leaves.

The common name comes from the plant's use as a wound herb in the 17th century and traditionally as a gargle for sore throats and mouth sores. It contains ursolic acid, which is a diuretic and has antitumor properties.

This plant can be found in most open areas, along roadsides and trails, and waste areas. Watch for mats of it in lawns.

Solanum dulcamara   June–September   Plate **27E**
Climbing Nightshade   Nightshade Family
    The most eye-catching attribute of climbing night-
shade is its bright red berries which often occur simul-
taneously with the dark violet flowers. The 1/2-inch
flowers have 5 backward-curving petals and a yellow
cone in the middle formed by fusion of the stamens.
The flowers occur in drooping clusters arising from the
internodes or opposite leaves. The leaves are alternate
and ovate, with pointed tips and often 1 or 2 basal lobes
or leaflets. They may be up to 3 1/2 inches long. The
branched stems climb or sprawl on other vegetation,
have woody bases, and may reach 10 feet in length.
    The juice has been used as a folk remedy for warts
and felons — inflammation of the finger or toe near the
nail. Nightshades contain solanine, which has narcotic
properties; they have been used to induce urination or
sweating. They can also cause vomiting, vertigo, convulsions, weakened heartbeat, and paralysis. Climbing
nightshade has been implicated in livestock poisonings.
This and related plants are used to make steroids and
have been shown to have anticancer activity.
    Many kinds of birds eat the seeds and probably are
the main agents for distributing the seed. The plant is
often found growing in the crotches of trees. It is an alternate host for tomato mosaic disease and should be
removed from areas around gardens. An introduction
from Europe, this species is found in moist areas
throughout the Berkshires.

Campanula rapunculoides   July–August   Plate **27F**
Rover Bellflower,
Creeping Bellflower   Bellflower Family
    Rover bellflower is one of the handsomest of introduced flowers, but it is cursed by many gardeners because of its invasiveness.

> *The most insatiable and irrepressible of beautiful weeds.
> If once its tall and arching spire of violet bells prevail
> on you to admit it to your garden, neither you nor its
> choice inmates will ever know peace again.*
> — Reginald Farrer, plant collector and eminent rock garden designer, 1880–1920

    The 1 1/2-inch purplish blue nodding bells with 5 lobes occur on a tall, mostly 1-sided slender terminal raceme. The leaves are alternate, stalked or sessile; the upper ones are lanceolate and the lower, heart shaped. The unbranched stalks may reach 3 feet tall.
    In Russia it has been used to treat hydrophobia.
    You will find creeping bell flower almost everywhere in the Berkshires where there has been a garden or home site.

Pontederia cordata   July–August   Plate **28A**
Pickerel Weed   Pickerel Weed Family
    Pickerel weed is easily identified by a combination of its flowers, leaves, and habitat. The flowers, violet blue, occur in dense terminal spikes 3 to 6 inches long. The 1/3-inch-wide flowers are funnel shaped with 2 lips, each with 3 lobes and with a yellow spot on the upper lip. A sheathlike bract clasps the stem just below the flower spike. A single leaf 4 to 10 inches long arises

from about the midpoint of the stem. It is shaped like an arrowhead, cordate at the base, tapering to a blunt tip, and the base of the petiole sheaths the stem. The stem may be 3 1/2 feet tall with the top 1 or 2 feet of the plant held above the water.

The young leaves are edible raw or cooked, fruits can be eaten raw or roasted and ground into flour, and the seeds may be eaten like nuts. Muskrats and several species of ducks eat the seeds.

Pickerel weed occurs in shallow water in marshes, ponds, and lakes.

Scutellaria galericulata   July–August   Plate **28B**
Marsh Skullcap   Mint Family

Skullcaps have 2-lipped flowers, the upper of which is shaped like a hood and the lower flaring with 3 lobes. Marsh skullcap flowers are blue, about 1 inch long, and occur singly in the leaf axils. The leaves are opposite, lanceolate, toothed, sessile or short-stemmed, and up to 5 inches long. The branched stems are square with fine hairs on the edges, and may reach 3 1/2 feet tall.

Herbalists have used this and related species as a nerve tonic and muscle relaxant.

Marsh skullcap is found wet areas in meadows and near water bodies. Look for it at Pleasant Valley Sanctuary, Canoe Meadows, Bartholomew's Cobble, and Notchview Reservation.

Mad-dog skullcap, *S. laterifolia*, is also found in the Berkshires. It has 1/2-inch-long blue flowers on 1-sided racemes arising from the leaf axils.

Verbena hastata   July–August   Plate **28C**
Blue Vervain, Simpler's Joy   Vervain Family

If you come upon a rather tall, coarse plant with terminal spikes of small purplish flowers in open areas in late summer, you may have found blue vervain. The 1/8-inch-wide flowers are tubular with 5 flaring petals and open from the bottom to the top of the spike. The leaves, which may reach 6 inches long, are lanceolate, with the lower ones often 3-lobed, and coarsely toothed. They are opposite on the branched stem which is square, grooved, and hairy, and may measure 5 feet tall.

Some American Indians roasted and ground the seed into flour and brewed a tea of the leaves to use as a female tonic. The seeds are eaten by birds, especially the swamp sparrow, *Melospiza georgiana*.

Blue vervain can be found in fields and pastures, woodsides, thickets, and along water bodies. It is common at Pleasant Valley Sanctuary and Bartholomew's Cobble.

Arctium minus   July–September   Plate **28D**
Common Burdock   Aster Family

Tenacious brown burs in a pet's fur or on one's socks are often the first introduction to common burdock. The flower heads look much like green versions of the burs with purplish tufts at the top. The heads occur in axillary clusters; they may be on short stalks or sessile. The bracts of the flower heads become the prickles that catch on clothing and fur. The leaves are alternate, heart shaped, rhubarblike, woolly underneath, with hollow stems, and may be up to 20 inches long. The stems are highly branched and may reach 5 feet tall.

Common burdock is a biennial introduced from

Europe. First-year plants are edible. Young leaves may be used fresh or cooked while roots and stems are usually cooked with a change of water to get rid of the bitter taste. A culinary variety is cultivated in Japan. It has been used as a tonic and diuretic. A poultice of fresh leaves can be used to treat poison ivy rash.

You will find common burdock in rich soil and neglected areas, especially along roadsides.

Cichorium intybus   July–September   Plate **28E**
Chicory, Blue Sailors   Aster Family

From midsummer through fall the bright blue (occasionally white, rarely pink) flowers of chicory are a familiar sight along roads and parking lots and in fields and pastures. Since the species does well in alkaline soils, it is at home in and near concrete. Chicory is a tall (up to 4 feet), stiff-looking relative of dandelion with similarly shaped flower heads and leaves. The ray flowers are square-tipped and fringed, the lower leaves are lobed or toothed, the upper ones are alternate and simple. The stalkless heads last only a day and close in cloudy weather; they make poor cut flowers.

The plant is widely used as food. The white underground portion of the leaf crown can be used as a salad green; Belgian endive is a cultivated variety of chicory. The upper leaves are very bitter and must be cooked with several changes of water to make them palatable. The root is ground and roasted as a coffee substitute or additive. It is also used in baked goods to intensify sugar flavor.

Cirsium arvense July–September Plate **28F**
Canada Thistle Aster Family

A large colony of thistles with numerous 1-inch-high lavender heads is probably Canada thistle. The heads are held in terminal and axillary clusters, and all the flowers on a given plant are male or female. The alternate leaves are mostly sessile, lanceolate with deeply cut, wavy, spiny-margined edges. The smooth stalks, branched near the top, may reach 5 feet tall.

This European species was introduced into Canada and from there into the United States. It is found in pastures, meadows, fields, and waste areas. It has been declared a noxious weed in 37 states. Eradication is difficult: when broken during cultivation, every piece of the rhizome will produce a new plant.

The leaves, when stripped of their spines, may be eaten raw or cooked, and the peeled stem may be used as a potherb. Milk in which the plant was boiled has been used to treat dysentery, and tea made from the leaves is a diuretic.

Canada thistle is a common plant in the Berkshires.

Epipactis helleborine July–September Plate **29A**
Helleborine, Weed Orchid Orchis Family

Watch for an upright plant 6 inches to 3 feet tall along trails and roads through wooded areas. The flowers are about 1/2 inch across, purple to greenish purple, not very showy, and borne on terminal racemes. The lower lip forms a small sac. It has alternate oval leaves which clasp the stem.

This is the only introduced species of orchid in North America. It appears to be spreading, perhaps because it is self-pollinating. This is probably the most abundant

orchid in our area. You are sure to find it at Bartholomew's Cobble, Kennedy Park, or Notchview Reservation,
and on Mount Greylock.

Dipsacus sylvestris   August   Plate **29B**
Teasel, Venus' Basin   Teasel Family
    Teasels are coarse, prickly plants with distinctive
flower clusters that add variety to the landscape year
round. The flowers are lavender, tubular, less than 1/2
inch long, and crowded in terminal, egg-shaped, bristly heads. The heads, which may be as long as 4 inches,
are subtended by several slender, pointed bracts. The
first flowers to open lie in a belt around the center of
the head, and then new ones open progressively in both
directions. The opposite leaves are lanceolate and
coarsely toothed, with prickles on the underside of the
midvein; they may reach 16 inches long. The leaves may
fuse at the base forming a cup (Venus' basin). The stiff
and prickly stems may reach 6 feet in height.
    Look for this introduction from Europe on roadsides
and in old fields and pastures. Teasel is often used in
dried flower arrangements.

Lobelia inflata   August   Plate **29C**
Indian Tobacco, Asthma Weed   Lobelia Family
    Indian tobacco has 1/4-inch tubular pale blue or lav-
ender flowers that are 2-lipped. The lower lip is 3-lobed
and bearded and the upper, 2-lobed. The flowers occur
singly in the axils of small leaves or bracts. The leaves
are alternate, ovate, toothed, and hairy underneath, and
may reach 2 1/2 inches long. The branched, hairy stems
may reach 1 1/2 feet tall.

Some American Indians dried the leaves and smoked them to treat asthma, bronchitis, and sore throat. The plant contains toxic substances. One, lobeline, is used commercially in quit-smoking lozenges and gum; it is said to appease the need of cigarette addicts for nicotine. Indian tobacco has been tied to human deaths and should never be used in self-treatment.

Indian tobacco is found throughout the Berkshires on roadsides and in open woods and meadows.

Monarda fistulosa   August   Plate **29D**
Wild Bergamot, Horsemint   Mint Family

Watch for a ragged, dense crown of lavender flowers. The individual flowers are tubular with 2 lips. The upper lip has 2 lobes and the lower, 3. The stamens protrude from the tubes. The gray green leaves are opposite and lanceolate to triangular with coarse-toothed margins. They have a spicy, minty odor. The leaves subtending the flower heads are often tinged with purple. The stem is square, erect, and often branched, and may reach 3 1/2 feet tall.

The leaves can be dried and used to make a fragrant tea. American Indians used the plant to treat a variety of ailments. True bergamot is a kind of sour orange. Wild bergamot is often used in perennial gardens and is a parent of many garden hybrids.

Watch for it in well-drained open areas in woods and fields. A big stand grows next to the parking lot at Bartholomew's Cobble.

Cirsium vulgare   August–September   Plate **29E**
Bull Thistle   Aster Family

Bull thistle is our spiniest thistle. The purple flower heads consist only of ray flowers and may be up to 2 inches wide. The heads occur at the ends of spiny branches. The leaves, which may be up to 12 inches long, are alternate, pinnately lobed with spiny margins, and are white and woolly underneath. The stems are armed with spiny ridges and may grow to 6 feet in height.

Anything as spiny as this plant must be protecting something good to eat, and indeed, this relative of artichokes is edible. The young leaves, stripped of their spines, are said to be delicious. The stems may be peeled and eaten raw or cooked. The fleshy roots may be eaten in their first year from fall through winter; they are sometimes dried and ground into a flour.

These robust plants, introduced from Eurasia, are frequently found in pastures, open fields, and waste places.

Lobelia siphilitica   August–September   Plate **29F**
Great Lobelia, Great Blue Lobelia   Lobelia Family

Great lobelia has bright blue 2-lipped flowers with white throats (the lower lip has 3 lobes and the upper, 2 lobes) in leafy terminal spikes. The plant may grow as tall as 5 feet but usually is no taller than 2 feet. The numerous alternate pointed leaves are 2 to 4 inches long. The seed capsules open at the top and the seeds are shaken out by the wind.

The plant contains toxic lobelines, which are alkaloids similar to nicotine. They have emetic and sedative properties. The plant was used by American Indians to treat syphilis, hence the specific name.

Great lobelia is found in moist woods and swamps as well as along streams and ponds. The species is threatened in Massachusetts, but plants can usually be found at Bartholomew's Cobble. Cultivated and self-sown plants are abundant at the Berkshire Botanical Garden. The species is widely cultivated and a white form is available.

Lythrum salicaria   August–September   Plate **30A**
Purple Loosestrife   Loosestrife Family
The beautiful vistas of red purple flowers seen along Berkshire roads and in nearly every wet area are colonies of purple loosestrife. It is hard to think of them as an environmental disaster, but this introduced species is rapidly crowding out native species in New England and across the country. Efforts to eradicate it have so far been unsuccessful.

The individual flowers are 1/2 to 3/4 inch wide and have 5 or 6 petals. They are clustered in leaf axils in the upper part of the plant. The flowers occur in three types, each with a different combination of stamen and pistil lengths. These differences are thought to facilitate cross-pollination, and a given plant has only one of the three possible flower types. The lanceolate leaves are opposite or in whorls of 3 and are sessile on the squarish, hairy stem. The plant is erect and may grow to 5 feet tall.

The Greeks used purple loosestrife for a hair dye. It has also been used as an astringent and a gargle to treat sore throats.

You will find this plant abundant in open wet areas throughout the Berkshires.

Thymus pulegioides   August–September   Plate **30B**
Wild Thyme, Mother of Thyme   Mint Family

You might first notice wild thyme when its herbal scent assails you as you crush it while sitting in an open area or weeding it from the edges of your garden. The flowers are purple, about 1/4 inch long, and in terminal spikes. The opposite leaves are oblong to ovate, entire, and short-stalked, and may reach 3/8 inch long. The stems are square and creeping, branched, and root at the nodes. The plant forms dense mats.

Wild thyme may be substituted for cultivated thyme as a culinary herb but is less flavorful. In European folk tradition, the leaves of wild thyme were used to brew a tea for nervous disorders, flu, stomachaches, and as an expectorant. American colonists used it to promote menstruation. Oil of thyme is an antispasmodic, lowers blood pressure, and increases heart rate. It is toxic and highly irritating to the skin. Thymol, the main active ingredient in oil of thyme, is used in antiseptics, mouthwashes, gargles, and toothpastes.

Wild thyme was introduced from Europe and is common in lawns and fields, and along roadsides. Thymes are highly variable plants, and their nomenclature has been quite confused. Many forms, including this one, have been called *T. serpyllum*. Many cultivated thymes are available with flowers in white or various shades of red, purple, or blue; some have variegated foliage. Choose plants that you like and don't worry about the correct names.

Aster cordifolius   August–October   Plate **30C**
Heart-leaved Aster, Blue Wood Aster   Aster Family

You will find many blue asters throughout the

Berkshires. If the lower or basal leaves are cordate (more or less heart shaped), are less than 3 inches wide, and don't clasp the stem, the plant you are trying to identify is probably this species. If the leaves clasp the stem it is *A. undulatum*, wave-leaved aster, and if the lower leaves are more than 3 inches wide, it is *A. macrophyllus*, large-leaved aster.

Heart-leaved aster is a quite variable species, measuring from about 1 foot to 4 feet tall with blue or violet ray flowers and yellow disk flowers in heads up to 3/4 inches wide in terminal clusters. This species is found in woods, clearings, and along trails and roads. Several species of blue-flowered asters can be used to produce yellow, orange, or green dyes.

Aster novae-angliae	September Plate **30D**
New England Aster	Aster Family

New England aster, our most showy wild aster, stands out among the many species of aster blooming in fall in the Berkshires because of its large (to 1 1/2-inch-wide) flower heads, deep purple ray flowers, and yellow orange disk flowers. The numerous heads have sticky bracts and stems. The alternate leaves are lanceolate, clasp the stem, and are covered with stiff hairs. The stems are erect and may reach 7 feet in height.

Some American Indians brewed a tea from the roots to treat diarrhea and fevers.

New England aster is common in fall along roadsides and in meadows and fields. The flowers may be dried and used in potpourris. The plant is commonly grown in perennial borders; cultivars with flowers in white and shades of pink, lavender, blue, and purple are available.

Gentiana clausa   September **30E**
Closed Gentian, Bottle Gentian   Gentian Family
     The flowers of closed gentian never open, and bees must force their way into them. They are blue, cylindrical, to 1 1/2 inches long, and occur in terminal clusters or in the upper leaf axils. The opposite leaves are lanceolate to oblong, pointed, sessile, and may reach 6 inches long; they form a whorl below the flowers. The stem is unbranched and may reach 2 1/2 feet tall.
     Closed gentian is found in wet meadows and thickets. Watch for it along Yokun Brook at Pleasant Valley Sanctuary.

Gentianopsis crinita   September–October   Plate **30F**
Fringed Gentian   Gentian Family
     Just when it seems that the flowering season has run its course, the gentians appear. Among the most beautiful and common is fringed gentian. The flowers are an intense violet blue, about 2 inches long, with 4 fringed lobes. They open only in the bright sun; otherwise the petals twist together to close.
     The flowers are solitary on erect branched stems. The leaves are opposite, oval to lanceolate, and sessile. The plants may grow to 2 feet tall.
     This species is the subject of Berkshire poet William Cullen Bryant's poem *To the Fringed Gentian* (1832).

> *Thou blossom bright with autumn dew,*
> *And colored with the heaven's own blue,*
> *That openest when the quiet light*
> *Succeeds the keen and frosty night.*

Fringed gentian will be found in moist areas in meadows and woods. Watch for it at Bartholomew's Cobble.

Green to Brown Flowers

Symplocarpus foetidus   April   Plate **32A**
Skunk Cabbage   Arum Family

Skunk cabbage is one of the earliest wildflowers to bloom in the Berkshires. As soon as the flower begins to develop, the respiratory rate of the plant accelerates and generates enough heat to keep the plant warmer than the surrounding air temperature. The heat generated is often sufficient to melt snow and ice. The purple brown hoods (spathes) of the plant appear before the leaves unroll, often while snow still covers the ground.

Each hood is shaped somewhat like a seashell, pointed at the top, and about 6 inches long. Inside it, many tiny pale purplish flowers cover a short column (spadix). If you get close enough to see them you will surely notice the foul odor given off to attract pollinators. The basal leaves are prominently veined, resemble those of cabbages, and may grow to 2 feet in length. If crushed they smell like skunk.

The leaves and rhizomes contain calcium oxalate crystals, which will cause a painful burning sensation if eaten fresh. The rhizomes when dried can be ground into a flour which is said to taste like cocoa. Some American Indians inhaled the scent of crushed leaves to dispel headaches. The seeds are eaten by ring-necked pheasants.

Skunk cabbage grows in wet areas and can often be seen along Berkshire roadsides. It is easy to find at Pleasant Valley Sanctuary and Bartholomew's Cobble.

Caulophyllum thalictroides   April–May   Plate **32B**
Blue Cohosh, Papoose Root   Barberry Family

In April, look for purple shoots with a waxy bloom a foot or more tall in moist woodlands. These are the first spring sign of blue cohosh. The brownish maroon to greenish yellow flowers appear before the triternate (3-times-ternate) compound bluish leaves are fully developed. In fall, the large dark blue, pea-sized seeds are held upright over the browning foliage.

The plant can cause dermatitis and is very irritating to the mucous membranes. It tastes extremely bitter and is avoided by livestock; the fruit and roots are poisonous. In spite of these properties or maybe because of them, American Indians and early colonists used blue cohosh to induce menstruation and childbirth.

Look for blue cohosh along the trails on Mount Greylock, Kennedy Park, and Bartholomew's Cobble.

Arisaema triphyllum   May   Plate **31**
Jack-in-the-Pulpit, Indian Turnip   Arum Family

An upright cone with an overarching flap (the "pulpit") enclosing a pale yellow club ("jack") make this plant unmistakable. The pulpit is a specialized bract, or spathe, while the jack is the actual inflorescence, or spadix. The tiny yellowish flowers clustered on the spadix may be male or female. Depending on age and growing conditions a given plant may bear male or female flowers. Sometimes this plant is divided into more than one species depending on the color (white, green, or purple) and extent of ribbing of the spathe. Examples of several kinds are found in our area. The leaves (usually only 1 or 2 per plant) occur on tall stalks up to 3 feet tall and end in 3 leaflets held above the pulpit. In late sum-

mer and fall, the flower stalks bear clusters of bright
red berries; these are often eaten by wild turkeys and
thrushes.

American Indians dried and ground the bulblike
root into flour. Fresh roots contain calcium oxalate crystals and cause intense burning if eaten.

Jack-in-the-pulpit is common in moist woods throughout our area.

Acorus calamus   June   Plate **32C**
Sweet Flag, Calamus   Arum Family
Plants in wet places which resemble iris but have a
conelike structure projecting from the side of a leaflike
stem are almost certainly sweet flag. The tiny greenish
yellow flowers densely cover the 2- to 3 1/2-inch spadix.
The long, narrow leaves arise from a basal clump and may
reach 4 feet in length. All parts of the plant are aromatic.

Sweet flag is found in marshes, swamps, wet ditches,
and the margins of ponds.

The young shoots, which are tender when less than
1 foot long, can be used in salads. The rhizome can be
boiled and candied. Cree Indians chewed the rhizome
as a strong stimulant and possibly as a hallucinogen.
The pleasant-smelling leaves have been strewn on floors
to suppress household odors. Asian strains of sweet flag
contain the carcinogen beta-asarone, thus the species is
classified by the USDA as unsafe. Nonflowering plants
are easily mistaken for the poisonous *Iris versicolor*, but
the latter is not aromatic.

Laportea canadensis   July–September   Plate **32D**
Wood Nettle   Nettle Family

The stinging hairs of nettles probably call attention to the plants more often than their inconspicuous flowers. The flowers are greenish, about 1/6 inch wide, and have no petals. They occur in dense, branching terminal and axillary clusters. The upper long, loose clusters consist of female (pistillate) flowers whereas the lower, smaller clusters consist of male (staminate) flowers. The leaves are alternate, stalked, ovate, and coarsely toothed. The stems are unbranched and appear to zigzag between the leaf nodes. The entire plant is covered with stinging hairs. The otherwise similar stinging nettle, *Urtica dioica* (see below), has opposite leaves.

Young plants can be cooked and eaten as greens.

Wood nettle is common throughout the Berkshires in moist woods and along the banks of streams.

Urtica dioica   July–September   Plate **32E**
Stinging Nettle   Nettle Family

If you spend much time in the woods, you may become more familiar with this plant than you would like to: the merest brush against it with bare skin will result in a sharp stinging sensation.

The greenish to cream flowers are tiny, less than 1/10 inch long. They have a 4-parted calyx but no petals and are either male or female. They occur in feathery, branched, drooping axillary clusters. The leaves are opposite, stalked, lanceolate and toothed, and may be up to 6 inches long. The stems, which are usually unbranched, may reach 6 feet or more in height. The entire plant is covered with stinging hairs.

The populations of stinging nettle in the Berkshires

may consist of native or introduced plants. As a rule, the native plants have flowers of both sexes on the same plant (monoecious), with the female flowers toward the top of the plant and male flowers lower down. Introduced plants usually have the sexes on different plants (dioecious). In addition, the base of the leaves is cordate. The two types of plants do not interbreed because they have different numbers of chromosomes.

The young shoots and leaves may be cooked and eaten as greens or used in soups and stews since cooking destroys the sting. They are rich in iron and vitamins C and A. The plant is sometimes used to flavor beer and is a commercial source of chlorophyll. Herbalists have used stinging nettle to treat ailments of the urinary tract, rheumatism, and gout. In Germany, the roots are used to treat prostate cancer and in Russia the leaves are used to treat inflammation of the gallbladder and hepatitis. In Europe, it is used for a hair rinse. The stem fibers can be used to make a fabric similar to linen; stinging nettle was once cultivated in Scotland for fiber. During World War I, wild plants were collected in Germany to make fabric for military uniforms. The plant can be used to make a green dye.

Stinging nettle is abundant in moist soil in the Berkshires in woodland borders and along trails and roadsides. You are sure to brush up against it somewhere. The stinging sensation can often be relieved by rubbing stinging areas with the stem of jewelweed, *Impatiens capensis* or *I. pallida* (see p. 64).

Ambrosia artemisiifolia   August–September   Plate **32F**
Ragweed   Aster Family
    A coarse plant of disturbed ground, ragweed can

be recognized by terminal and axillary racemes of inconspicuous greenish flowers. The lower leaves are opposite and the upper ones alternate; they are finely dissected and may be up to 4 inches long. The stems are hairy. Ragweed is an annual and is eventually crowded out by perennials such as goldenrod.

Ragweed is wind-pollinated and produces great quantities of airborne pollen. Ragweeds are the major cause of hay fever in North America. They also cause contact dermatitis in some individuals. The seeds are rich in oil and are an important food for mourning doves, bobwhites, wild turkeys, red-winged blackbirds, snow buntings, American goldfinches, dark-eyed juncos, horned larks, common redpolls, fox sparrows, song sparrows, white-crowned sparrows, white-throated sparrows, and rufous-sided towhees, among other species.

You will have no trouble finding ragweed in cultivated fields, construction sites, along roads, and in cracks in parking lots and sidewalks.

REFERENCES

Brown, Paul Martin. *A Field and Study Guide to the Orchids of New England and New York*. Jamaica Plain, Massachusetts: Orchid Press, 1994.

Buchanan, Rita. *A Weaver's Garden*. Loveland, Colorado: Interweave Press, 1987.

Cox, Donald D. *Common Flowering Plants of the Northeast*. Albany: State University of New York Press, 1985.

Elias, Thomas S., and Peter A. Dykeman. *Field Guide to North American Edible Wild Plants*. New York: Outdoor Life Books, 1982.

Foster, Steven, and James A. Duke. *A Field Guide to Medicinal Plants*. Boston: Houghton Mifflin, 1990.

Gleason, Henry A., and Arthur Cronquist. *Manual of Vascular Plants of Northeastern United States and Adjacent Canada*. 2d ed. Bronx: New York Botanical Garden, 1991.

Lampe, Kenneth F., and Mary Ann McCann. *AMA Handbook of Poisonous and Injurious Plants*. Chicago: American Medical Association, 1985.

Laubach, René. *A Guide to Natural Places in the Berkshire Hills*. Stockbridge, Massachusetts: Berkshire House, 1992.

Lewis, Walter H., and Memory P. F. Elvin-Lewis. *Medical Botany*. New York: John Wiley & Sons, 1977.

Martin, Alexander C., Herbert S. Zim, and Arnold L. Nelson. *American Wildlife and Plants*. New York: Dover Publications, 1961.

McGrath, Anne. *Wildflowers of the Adirondacks*. Utica, New York: North Country Books, 1981.

McVaugh, Rogers. *Flora of the Columbia Country Area, New York*. Albany: Bulletin Number 360. New York State Museum and Science Service, 1957.

Moyle, John B., and Evelyn W. Moyle. *Northland Wildflowers*. Minneapolis: University of Minnesota Press, 1977.

Niering, William A., and Nancy C. Olmstead. *The Audubon Society Field Guide to North American Wildflowers*. Eastern Region. New York: Alfred A. Knopf, 1979.

Newcomb, Lawrence. *Newcomb's Wildflower Guide*. Boston: Little, Brown, 1977.

Reader's Digest. *Magic and Medicine of Plants*. Pleasantville, New York: The Reader's Digest Association, 1986.

Stevens, Lauren. *Hikes & Walks in the Berkshire Hills*. Stockbridge, Massachusetts: Berkshire House, 1990.

Weatherbee, Pamela A. "Flora of Berkshire County, Massachusetts." Master's thesis, University of New Hampshire, 1990.

INDEX TO COMMON
AND SCIENTIFIC NAMES